My Teachable Moments

Stories of a High School Science Teacher

Dr. Shannon W. McPherson

My Teachable Moments

Stories of a High School Science Teacher

Dr. Shannon W. McPherson

Copyright ©2024 Dr. Shannon W. McPherson

Neuroplasticity Publishing

Cover design by Pankaj Singh Renu

Edited by Tamelynda Lux

First Printing

ISBN: 979-8-9897371-0-9

shannonwmcpherson@gmail.com

www.docmcpherson.com

This book is dedicated to my partner in life, Paul, my supportive, loving family, and all the students that I have learned from throughout the years.

My Teachable Moments

Stories of a High School Science Teacher

Howdy reader! My name is Dr. Shannon McPherson, but my students call me "Doc." I'd like to think I'm still sane after teaching science in public high schools for almost half my life. Twenty-six years of experiencing the highs and lows of teenagers as a trusted teacher takes a toll on the mind.

I have taught in four different high schools in four separate school districts, all with quite diverse student bodies and administration styles. The educational objectives of these districts and institutions varied in terminology, each with the same basic premise to ensure student success.

I love my students and am passionate about my chosen profession, but I'm on the precipice of a career change due to vast issues with public education. Between the changes in student behavior after COVID-19, manipulating colleagues, and an unrealistic and ill-equipped administration, I am struggling with the change.

As with every job, there have been positive and negative experiences. I have encountered both extremely demotivating and unfavorable situations and incredibly stimulating and positive administration.

I decided to write this book to examine and explain why I teach after being prodded by family and friends to share my stories and teachable moments. If I do leave public education, will I still be considered trustworthy, genuine, humorous, and mindful? Can I still provide a safe space with a collegiate vibe? Can I use the same techniques with college students as I do with teenagers? Can I do the same with an online audience of students?

Throughout these pages, you will read student stories and my own stories as experienced over a twenty-six-year career. I hope you will laugh with me, cry with me, and step into my shoes as I relive the stories of the students I have been honored to educate and the different administrators who affected me and my learners throughout the years. The trials and tribulations are vast, as are the aha and meaningful educational moments.

Table of Contents

Chapter 1

Organized Chaos

"What the heck? Really? Seriously? No, no, no, no! Don't lick the rat! Give him his money back. No, you may not pay him to lick the rat!"

Welcome to high school science. Yes, I'm the teacher. And yes, this has been said more times than I can count about rats, mice, brains, eyeballs, blue liquids, green liquids, digested food, and, well, you get the idea. Most normal people would become irritated and discouraged with students who try such silly antics, but not me. I LOVE IT. I don't love that they want to lick inappropriate things in class. I love the hilarity of it.

Students' high school shenanigans keep me on my toes, running from here to there, usually laughing or cursing under my breath. Sometimes both, at the same time.

I have been teaching for twenty-six years, having taken off a year here and there due to burnout. But until recently, I have always assumed that I would wind up back in front of a high school classroom. Did you catch that? I said, "Until recently." I've always had a passion for teaching, and not just for the subject that I teach.

As a high school science teacher, I have taught a vast arsenal of subject material: chemistry, environmental science, biology, anatomy, and physiology, as well as advanced and college levels of some of these courses. I've also taught specialized subjects such as medical microbiology, pathophysiology, the principles of health science technology, and medical terminology. These courses are specifically designed for young adults entering the medical field or medical sciences.

Students heading into the medical field are stoic in their learning, so it tends to take time for them to open up and be themselves due to the self-induced stress they are under. As each year progressed in these classes, the students learned that I accepted their individual traits and talents.

For example, I agreed they should be thankful for mitochondria when they wrote that word on a thankfulness banner I placed in class. They also learned

I would laugh with them as they learned to use matches to light alcohol burners in medical microbiology. I was amazed to discover that only two of the twenty medical microbiology students had ever used matches. The students were mesmerized by the spark, smell, and instant fire that erupted from a simple kitchen match.

One girl absolutely loved striking the match and routinely asked to have the matches to show her friends outside class. I found her curiosity both concerning and wonderful, but I instinctively knew I had to put the classroom matches under lock and key. I am glad to say she seems to have gotten over her match obsession, according to her recent TikTok videos.

After working in four different school districts, I have seen a lot at different high schools with 2,500–4,000 students on campus. And I mean a lot! From wealthy suburban schools to schools with over 80 percent of the student population in the free and reduced lunch program. I have experienced a plethora of interesting situations. This includes students, fellow teachers, and administrators. All gambits have been endured. Good, mediocre, lackluster, and borderline evil have been imprinted into my mind.

At one point in my career, I transferred to a different school district and chose to teach at an inner-city high school and I was concerned that my teaching style would not be appreciated when I arrived. My teaching style is a hybrid mix of facilitator and coach. A facilitator promotes self-learning and the growth of critical thinking skills, while a coach includes an abundance of hands-on activities. In addition, I was anxious about the difficulties I could face due to the lack of similarities with the children. I'm glad to report that I was mistaken. The same hunger for knowledge filled their eyes, and I was ready to feed them the knowledge they craved.

While at this campus, I learned new ways to approach difficult concepts by continuously assessing their prior knowledge and providing constant feedback to increase self-esteem and develop positive relationships. Looking back, I appreciate that period of my life, and I will forever love those kids.

Like any business, supportive administration can guide you as an educator on your worst day and destroy you on your best day. I shall try my best to refrain from describing various forms of administration an teaching styles by not using overused educational buzzwords such as growth mindset, best practices, engagement, grit, rigor, differentiation, lifelong learning, scaffolding, etc. I assume you don't want to read another how-to-teach book. There are plenty on the market, and that is not the purpose of my writing this book.

Honestly, the last few years in the classroom have been hard—really hard. I mean, running barefoot through a fire-ant-hill kind of hard. After COVID-19, kids have become complacent, school administrators have micromanaged the school climate, and colleagues don't seem to share or collaborate as before the pandemic. Data feels as if it is hoarded away in the cloud, shrouded by passwords, and resources feel as if they are stored behind locked doors. In addition, everyone is terrified of saying anything that could be misconstrued in any way, and rules have become increasingly rigid regarding what can and can't be discussed and taught in the classroom.

Due to new legislation in my state, I can't teach how the reproductive system works, although it is state-mandated that I do since I teach advanced and dual credit anatomy and physiology. I have never gone into the "Bow Chicka Wow Wow" version of how a baby is made, but I am not allowed to teach the subject matter without parental consent. What the hell? I was shocked when I learned that I would have to kill a few trees for the paperwork to be signed by parents to discuss this vitally important part of the curriculum.

As you read this book, I will share how it feels to be an educator who cares deeply for their students and how that has resulted in student achievement, whatever that may look like for that individual. Learners reap results we can never fully understand, which is part of the educator experience. Of course, you know that already, don't you?

For some time, I taught at a school that specialized in career and technology classes: culinary, pharmacy tech, cosmetology, automotive tech, and veterinary tech. Classes were short (about forty minutes each) since the students had to travel from their campus to ours during the school day. There was a small group of kids who stayed at our campus all day, choosing the family-like atmosphere. They were the only students on campus for about an hour each day.

Russ, a blond-headed rascal of a junior, still stands out in my mind, and we have stayed in touch through social media. My classroom was a fishbowl, with windows on the sides for observers to watch the madness in my classroom. Okay, not madness in the sense of unrestrained, but controlled chaos.

Russ would show up early each day with the sole purpose of posing a skeleton in the windows of my classroom. Schoolmates entered the building adjacent to these windows and always enjoyed what he did. Sometimes, he created big productions involving dresses, wigs, and sunglasses. On other days, the skeleton would be posed with just a hat on its head. It brought Russ joy, so I let him do it. I knew that his mother had not been readily present in his life for a while, and he needed to be appreciated and encouraged to be himself. He was a witty, smart-mouthed kid with a crazy sense of humor who spent most of his free time in my room, quietly studying or talking my ears off. Russ didn't have a medium power setting.

I will share the difficulties arising from a lack of administration support. Many years ago, I taught advanced biology and loved taking my students to the zoo in the spring to research endangered animals. The field trips had always been approved, and the students were always willing to pay for the buses and entry fees. A new administrator had advanced up the chain of command, and without rhyme or reason, she denied the field trip. The trip was relevant, curriculum-based, content-aligned, differentiated, allowed incredible engagement, and encompassed best practices. She simply did not want the students to go on a field trip, and they were very disappointed. I tried to discuss this with her, but she refused to have a conversation with me about it. I left teaching for one year after that—she was clearly on a roll to inhibit creative teaching approaches.. Thus, she enjoyed micromanaging many of the more innovative educators, including myself, on campus. Wait, did I just use educational buzzwords? Sorry about that.

I will share how a positive administration can help faculty and staff do their best. I've had good administrators who are prompt, answer phone calls and emails, and support both the pupils and me—administrators who truly care about the kids and the soul of their school. They are conscientious and cognizant of the overall outcome, something educators refer to as student success. The administration at that campus was supportive and kind but very strict about hours, dress, and expectations. During this period of my educational career, I excelled at trying new and innovative things. Chemistry involved measuring tire pressure, cooking eggs without a stove, and allowing the students to make fudge based on chemical units of measure called moles. Students in my classroom learned that chemistry was not just a subject they had to pass; it was required for life.

A graduated college student who had been in my chemistry class sent me a message on Facebook. "I work in retail now, so I work with many high school kids, and they tell me when they're struggling, especially in chemistry. I remember that I was the only one of my friends who passed that class. I took chemistry with you at the career campus, and they all took it at our home school. I always told them that I had the best teacher ever because you really took the time to explain everything to us from top to bottom, and you made it fun!"

Bingo—isn't that the point of the twelve-hour days, weekends working into the wee hours of the night, and endless hours of grading?

In contrast, I've had administrators who do not respond to emails or prefer talking in person or on the phone during instructional time. That may be all well and good, but I need an email stream to remind me of our conversations. Educating over 100 teenagers per day will cause a strain on even the best and biggest of brainiacs. Plus, I like my pertinent information to be in writing, not gleaned from a short-winded and whispered conversation in the hallway outside my classroom while class is in session!

Like the kids aren't trying to listen to the conversation.

Seriously, how is this an acceptable way to converse about professional matters? In such an environment, my passion for the classroom dips to dangerously low levels, and it feels like I can't function properly.

If you are an educator with either of the above types of administrators, you know exactly how good it can feel or how horrid it can turn your day. For example, there was the time when a principal stated that his door was always open to discuss concerns but turned me away when his advice was needed, despite having an appointment with him.

The students feel it, too. High schoolers know when it is safe to be themselves. They thrive in an environment with bona fide authenticity, random humor, daily accountability, and avid learning, all wrapped up in a big red bow or whatever your school colors are.

One of my sweet seniors would usually enter my classroom with a confident bounce in his step, but one day, he entered with turned-down shoulders and a worried look. He had lost his mother the previous school year due to cancer and now lived with his elderly grandmother. He was kind, wanted to go to medical school, and wanted to make the world a better place, but he felt lost on this particular day. Another faculty member had berated him in front of his peers and constantly harassed him for the time he was in their classroom. The woman who treated him this way was known for her use of anger, aggression, and browbeating techniques in the classroom. I asked him what I could do to help, and he responded, "Nothing," as he stared out into space. This broke my heart. Why is it necessary to demean those you have committed to guide? They become downtrodden and display antagonism, pessimism, and basic teenagerly behavior.

My skills are not perfect; I'll never claim that, but I do have plenty of experience due to my conscious sharpening of the skills to have a peaceful, enlightened classroom. Unfortunately, several of my peers chose to bully and strong-arm their students daily. I suppose it was a power contest full of strife and exertion.

"You feel strongly about that, don't you?" This is a statement I made to a student in class recently. I followed up with, "Let's keep discussing alternate solutions to vaccinations and medical testing on humans and animals." Ryana felt very strongly about using animals as test subjects for medical purposes. Instead, she felt that prisoners and others beneath a prosperous society should be used to test such procedures. Ryana felt she could express her opinions in a safe environment; after all, she had me as an instructor for two different classes over two school years. This led to a long discussion with most of the class involved.

Allowing open discourse leads to a safe environment where respect is earned and praised. During Ryana's junior year, she was very shy and quiet during class. Big brown eyes chewed and digested every one of my words, and over time, her simple questions became more and more detailed. She was a highly intelligent and persistent schoolgirl who had found a trustworthy adult to converse with about topics commonly opposed by others.

These are the moments I wish my administration would take the time to observe to show how a safe environment can be cultivated to allow discussions to progress.

All this takes constant diligence on the educator's part to work toward a positive learning environment. It also requires support from colleagues, staff, management, and administration. Without advocation from the higher echelons of education, the school atmosphere and classroom, by extension, can become toxic, negative, and a place any person would not want to be. Throughout the years, I've had students tell me stories about teachers who are rude, inconsiderate, and bullish. I've never understood this behavior and have strived to provide a friendly room. A classroom where high expectations are kept but in a compassionate manner. Oh yeah, did I mention humor? High expectations with humor will win the day—any day.

I remember the conversation quite clearly: "Dude, you will let us do that?" John, an imaginative boy, and his industrious buddy wanted an aquaponics lab set up in the advanced placement environmental science class I was teaching. We were growing lettuce in the classroom, and I allowed the students to create their own lab experiments. Ultimately, we would have a salad party to eat the lettuce they had all successfully grown.

Between you and me, I sure hoped there would be plenty of successfully grown lettuce, or I would have to purchase salad-making supplies. I had equipment for them to use, for which I always supplied the basics for the populace. I never assumed that students could financially provide the needed materials.

I was highly intrigued by this project, so I used a bit of budget money to buy a few extra supplies. John and his lab partner monitored the chemistry, fish, water filtration, and everything else involved in this experiment. I let the kids choose what they wanted to do to be successful. To this day, he says it was one of the most meaningful experiences he had in high school. These two boys received the trust, sincere assistance, and unwavering support they were used to in my classroom.

The administration was very supportive at this school. I was allowed to grow my creativity, be supported, and be shown respect for my position and work. For instance, I was given my own budget to pay for supplies for my class. Nearly anything was acceptable if it was used as part of the curriculum. I was trusted to determine my lessons based on state requirements, compare costs, and purchase exactly what I needed to ensure student achievement. Many of my lab supplies can be purchased at local grocery stores, and most of what I bought was never questioned. (On a side note, this was the school where my students just started calling me by my single "star-studded" nickname, Doc. I even have a domain name honoring this nickname, www.docmcpherson.com.)

In contrast to the supportive administration mentioned above, my budget requests were continuously questioned at a different school district. I had to provide the exact learning outcome and how the items correlated to state-mandated knowledge with lesson plans and written justifications for nearly every expense. This was time-consuming and counterproductive to enhancing my students' learning since I spent an excessive amount of time managing the budget I was assigned. Honestly, I was reticent to be creative with activities because I could only purchase supplies from certified vendors, regardless of the cost. This made me feel as if my professionalism was being questioned.

As you read this memoir from a devoted teacher, I invite you to laugh, cry, and imagine yourself in my position. I will be reliving the stories of the students I have had the honor to teach, as well as the various administrators who have impacted me and my students over the years. As an extension, you will experience how students experienced hands-on learning in unique ways and how active mindfulness played a role in my classroom.

The aha moments and significant learning experiences are numerous, as are the challenges and tribulations.

Let's take a look at how a beautiful garden was brought to life with young people full of vigor and love, which eventually led to a change of mindset as a new future was planted despite an administration mottled with confusion and strife.

"The function of education is to teach one to think intensively and to think critically... Intelligence plus character – that is the goal of true education."

~ Martin Luther King Jr.

Chapter 2

Gardening

In your mind's eye, imagine humans working in tandem as they volunteer on a warm spring morning to create a beautiful, nearly sacred space for people, plants, and animals to live, thrive, and play. Fantasize the many smells such as savory sage, sweet mint, and spicy society garlic intermingled with a slight breeze. The sun shines down upon the freshly tilled soil, new planter boxes, and hundreds of donated bags of organic soil and compost.

I opened my eyes as I heard a grunt, a mass of giggles, and a girl saying, "Ewww, that's gross." I turned my head toward the laughter and spied a group of fifteen-year-olds running away from one of the boys. He was preparing to fling a handful of soft, moist compost. One of the girls ran toward me, hiding behind my five-foot frame, yelling, "Doc! Doc! Are we going to make gardens out of rotten food? That's so nasty!" She ducked down as the ball of soil and compost whizzed past her head, and small brown pellets landed on my shoulder. All I could do was laugh a deep, hearty, soul-bending laugh.

Several student-run groups had collected supplies in anticipation of this first full day of digging garden beds, placing the planters in place, and filling them with healthy organic soil. The Environmental Club, Health Occupations Students of America, Student Council, and numerous faculty and staff donated tomato cages, tools, hoses, seeds, soil, and garden gloves. The environmental classes had submitted grant proposals to access funds to build, plant, and maintain the new life that would thrive in this space. This Friday was Good Friday, and yes, it was an amazingly exhausting good Friday.

Within a year, the garden had become a lush, green paradise full of flowers, small fruit trees, vegetables, and herbs blended with native pollinators such as bees and butterflies. Small peaches had ripened, jalapenos had grown, big juicy figs were ready to taste, sweet watermelon, summer squash, tasty green beans, prickly okra, and fully harvestable bright red tomatoes were ready to eat.

Did I mention the wildflowers scattered among the rows? Junior gardeners instinctively knew not to step in these patches of wonderment.

My class surrounded me as I instructed them to close their eyes and become aware of the life surrounding them. A ninth-grade student felt a monarch butterfly wing whistle past her ear as it stopped for a snack on its migration route. Her face was flushed with excitement, and she began to bounce up and down in anticipation of learning more. Questions were thrown at me like darts toward a board. "How do they know there is food here?" "How do they know where to go and when to migrate?" "How can you tell a boy from a girl?" "What do they do in the summer?" An impassioned discussion began as my tribe was enraptured. We discussed a monarch butterfly's life cycle and growth process versus a black swallowtail or gulf fritillary. This set them off on a chase as they gently and lovingly looked through the bushes and host plants to discover eggs and caterpillars of various species.

Teenagers usually stare at small, portable screens for entertainment, which is a constant struggle in this age of technology. These kids had put up their phones and were beginning to experience the relationships of our natural world, a spiderweb of life, experimenting with growth, composting, renewal, and reuse of resources. They expressed incredible pride in their masterpiece and would share that joy with anyone who would listen.

Over six years, the school garden had grown with many donations, grants, and upkeep by classmates and faculty. It was an oasis dedicated to the love of learning. Art classes employed it as a place to craft their handiwork, and the wood shop used it to create a seating area as a memorial to a fallen staff member; photography classes created amazing artistry as they learned how to use camera equipment, chemistry classes tested the soil, culinary concocted incredible meals with the organic herbs grown, special education students utilized the space as a place to grow their own goodies to snack upon, and lunch goers used it as a calm place to eat their meals. Many marveled when first tasting a fresh vegetable off of the plant in the garden.

Imagine their surprise when they truly realized that food didn't have to come in a plastic package.

My favorite memory from this time frame was when I showed Noah that he could eat raw okra straight from the plant. His eyes lit up as he tasted the sweetness, and he ran to one of his buddies to share his newfound snack. Later, I found out that he began picking broccoli, okra, peaches, bite-sized tomatoes, and green beans and sharing them with his friends through the windows of classrooms nearby. I had wondered what happened to the produce we had been growing!

I ran into Noah at a local restaurant a few years after he graduated. A stranger had sent a drink to my husband and me, and of course, we both looked around to see who it was. A bearded, strong, charismatic man approached our table, saying loudly, "Doc?" Neither of us recognized this person, and we were a bit bewildered. After a few moments, I realized who it was. We gave each other big hugs and then visited for a bit. Noah shared that some of his favorite high school memories were spent in the garden. He had been part of the original group of students that built it, and he planned to build his own miniature version when he purchased his first house. We spoke of okra, tomatoes, dirt, broccoli, and how much he learned during those formative years of his life.

This is what happens when you have administrative support at all levels. This is what education should look like. This is what educational empowerment tastes like. Imagine school and district administration supporting you and your students as you experiment with different, clever, and innovative approaches to educating our youth and our future. This is what transpired at one campus for many years. Sigh. I miss the magic of that time.

Pray tell, what happened? Well, let's visualize it a little further. By the time I finish this story, you may lose your lunch.

Imagine that the original "head" administrator who supported your faculty, staff, and all students at your school was replaced by a bean counter, a real "numbers" guy, a data-driven person who required everything that occurred on campus to have quantifiable justification. Simply put, if you couldn't repetitively analyze data to a degree that made you want to vomit, he didn't approve. He and his cronies didn't approve of the garden and what it represented. They were more concerned with lawn maintenance.

Nope, I'm not kidding.

Despite documentation of approval for the campus improvement and that district guidelines and rules had been followed throughout the years, the newly placed upper ranks of the school district administration were hell-bent on removing the garden. I provided solutions to their perceived problems, pupils and parents wrote letters to the school board, and yes, I demanded to be involved in the unannounced meetings and decision-making that was going on behind the scenes. The team of bravados required that the garden be rebuilt to allow 100 percent of all special needs students access.

They had access! They had their own garden beds, which the boys and girls had built just for that specialized program!

My indoor classroom didn't even have 100 percent special needs access.

Tearful meetings ensued with the administration. Despite testimony from many individuals, including special education teachers, I was informed that the district would be removing the garden. I'm sure a few expletives were uttered under my breath as I strode away with my head held high, shoulders pulsing due to stifled emotion.

The day that maintenance from across the district opened the gates and drove past my classroom windows with a tractor and trailer, I knew that this was a battle I could not win despite all my efforts. No, I did not sit idly by as they destroyed and killed everything that we had worked for. I was a ball of spitfire energy as I raced out of my room to the scene of their crime and demanded that they stop destroying our creation until all was settled. Yes, I did manage to scare the roaches away that day.

Within three months, the six years of toil, labor, and love were demolished. The district had officially rescinded its garden approval, and I tearfully scheduled a day of gentle removal.

In December of that year, we removed the garden. Approximately sixty people showed up in frigid temperatures to salvage what could be saved. Plants were divided and shared, memories were made, and tears were shed.

I died inside. Every time I walked through that part of the school, my blood pressure would rise, my hands would clench, and my heart would race. The anger, pain, and anguish experienced as the garden was lost were felt by students, faculty, staff, and the critters who depended on that garden for survival. Heck, it still affects me this way... I just wiped away a tear from my computer keyboard.

So why stay? Why continue? What's the point if you will be shot in the foot each time you do the right thing for your students and your community? Why? Why, you say? The answer is simple. Hope. The hope is that the next day will be better, brighter, loving, and full of laughter.

The timing of the loss of the garden was interesting because it led to an advancement of my career in a different direction, into the world of career and technology education. At the time, I had been revamping my résumé and actively seeking jobs that could be fulfilling and meaningful. My commitment to serve my fellow man is a deep-seated part of my soul, and any employment I undertake must serve that purpose.

A seed of hope to stay in education was planted by a new and openly thinking administrator. She asked if I would expand my certification to include a health science certification, which would require a great deal of preparation and test-taking. The very administration that played a role in breaking my heart when the garden was lost asked for my assistance in this endeavor, an attestation to the faith they had in my abilities.

A new stage of my career emerged due to my willingness to expand health science opportunities for students who needed such classes. A new day was born, and my life as an educator continued as I agreed to accept the challenge.

"Free the child's potential, and you will transform him into the world."

~ Maria Montessori

Chapter 3

Why and How?

Julie ran into class, face flushed red, cafeteria breakfast sandwich in one hand, chocolate milk balanced in the other, with her phone falling out of her purse. "Doc, I'm so sorry I'm late. I hate being late! But the traffic, the cars. People are so stupid!" She sat with a humph in her seat and promptly put her head on her desk on the edge of tears as she tried to catch her breath.

I knew quite a bit about Julie's history. She was on the free lunch program; she was very active in many clubs, including more than one National Honor Society, and worked nearly full-time to help her parents pay the bills. She worked frantically hard in school to escape the lifestyle she had been raised in. She couldn't wait to get out of the house and on her own, so she could only be responsible for herself instead of being responsible for her parents and siblings. I greatly respected this child during such a tumultuous time of her life.

How does a professionally trained, compassionate, genuine, safe, and mindful educator handle this obvious sign of need? How does one help when a teenager signals for help?

SCREECH! HALT! This is NOT a how-to book like Robert J. Marzano's *Classroom Instruction that Works* or Harry and Rosemary Wong's *The First Days of School*. It is a book of stories from the front lines of a public high school science teacher who is weighing her potential options. It is not a guide to how to handle students with needs, whether real or perceived. It is definitely not a book on how to create kind, safe, and genuine classrooms. It is also not a wish list of innovative personality traits an administrator wants to see in their faculty.

It is a precautionary tale explaining why teachers leave the profession despite an incredible passion for their chosen career. It is also a book describing the difficulty in choosing to leave service to our youth, as these pages have turned into such a tale through heartfelt stories.

Recently, I sent a request across social media—Facebook for older students and Instagram for younger students. I have TikTok and Twitter accounts, but only to follow my twenty-six-year-old influencer daughter. I wanted to remember and know what memorable experiences students and colleagues recollected from time spent with me. Hundreds of responses were received, from over twenty years ago to the more recently graduated. I was greatly surprised by the themes I saw in their responses. Words used repeatedly included safe, fun, kind, compassionate, caring, genuine, passionate, and excited.

Why do I bring up these descriptors? I take great pride in being ascribed these traits. I am a realist and know that there are probably just as many derogatory terms being used regarding my personality and career, but I will leave that out of these pages!

Compassion, creativity, and openness allow students to take charge of their education, and I feel it is of prime importance to instill these traits each and every day in the classroom. This requires making connections with students of all ages, even when more than twenty-five students are crammed into a smallish space. All shapes, sizes, and backgrounds can be empowered to learn, utilize that knowledge, and still feel safe to make mistakes. A teacher's passion, love, and outpouring of support for the students in their care can teach those same students to be responsible for their educational experience. This is possible if the teacher expresses unconditional acceptance, displays respect, and loves what they do. Yes, being an educator can be great fun and incredibly satisfying, but it can also be stressfully exhausting.

Stop for a moment now and think of the years you spent in school. If you had the opportunity to spend time with one of your teachers from your formative years, who would it be? Why? Was it the way they made you feel? Did you feel safe being yourself? What are some of the personality and professional traits of that teacher that helped you feel empowered to learn?

Here is a short breakdown of the different aspects of my teaching style, based on graduated student responses on Facebook and Instagram, along with a few that I've thrown in that are vitally important to this journey I'm experiencing. I will briefly describe each topic in the remaining sections of this chapter and expand on them in the upcoming chapters. Along the way, you will be entertained as we explore accounts and stories of my experiences with students, colleagues, and administrators.

- Be Worthy of Trust
- Be a Genuine Person
- Humor is Healthy
- Mindfulness Journey
- Safety and Refuge
- Lab Coats, Paint, and Creative Problem Solving
- Collaborating with Counterparts
- School Administrative Stewardship

Be Worthy of Trust

Folks feel cozy and safe when they know what to expect. My teaching style sets guidelines and expectations in stone on the first day of school. Yes, I said, "in stone." And yes, I said the very first day. Rules and organized structures are vitally important for classroom management, overall mood, and forming bonds with students.

On the first day of class, I always meet the students at the door, assign them a seat, and explain what they are to do while they wait for me to start class. The first day of school is nerve-wracking for students since they don't know what to envision before setting foot in any classroom. When they are warmly welcomed with kind eyes and a genuine smile, they start to feel safe and begin to understand that you are a trusted adult.

When I asked you to recall a teacher from your school years, did you think about that teacher who was special to you? Did they smile and welcome you with open arms into their domain? Did they clearly state their expectations? Did they make you laugh? Did they truly care about your success? Or did you think of an educator who appeared to have bipolar disorder? Did they disrespect you terribly on one day and behave sweetly the next? Did they expect you to know the rules without verbalizing them? I don't know about you, but not knowing if someone will be harsh or pleasant makes me anxious. Just imagine how it would feel to be a teenager with wild hormones and an underdeveloped brain.

This reminds me of Jessica, who preferred to be called Jess. She was a spicy, communicative, redheaded senior who attended multiple classes in my classroom for two years. After students were required to return to in-person learning post COVID-19, she felt unsafe in the cafeteria during lunch. She asked if she could eat in my room since it was clean and exuded a calm atmosphere. During our shared lunches, we enjoyed discussions involving positive and negative adventures with other teachers. According to Jess, her first-period teacher was quite rigid and rarely interacted directly with his students. Jess would wave her arms and dance across the room as she explained how her peers would perform silly antics to get this teacher to respond. I'll always remember her red hair flying around her face and her hands waving around as she mimicked the craziness that occurred daily in that class.

Trust requires integrity, honesty, and consistency. Like Jess, students knew they could depend on me to be professional, discrete, and accountable. In exchange, I expected that of the students as well.

I can trust, they can trust, we can all trust!

Be a Genuine Person

What does that phrase mean? Genuine means to be actual, true, sincere, and honest. How does this apply to teenagers? They can sniff you like a dog and determine your nature. They can feel whether you are honest and authentic. Our youth instinctively know real fairness, empathy, compassion, and kindness. I'm not talking about being a pushover. I have had very high expectations for my pupils, sometimes a bit too lofty. As part of developing my teaching methods, I learned to tame those expectations by stepping back and regrouping my thoughts on the assignment or topic. This didn't require analyzing intricate data. It involved being authentic, genuine, and real. Did I give them too much information to digest? Could I find a new way to demonstrate the topic? Was there an activity they could perform to help them internalize and use the material covered?

Reality dictates that we must be malleable in our school climates to reach our students and bring about a larger impact on their future. Genuine teachers are honest and truly care about their students—emotionally, encouragingly, and, at times, creatively. My students knew I would be truthful—both professionally and respectfully.

On a side note, I have always had difficulty controlling my facial expressions, which was and still is quite funny. That usually led to humor.

Humor is Healthy

Ahhh, humor. What would this world be like without laughter? Think about it. How dull and drab our lives would be without chuckles, chortles, or giggling. I find humor easy to come by and use as a motivational tool since it can help students learn or remember difficult concepts. For example, during my first year of teaching chemistry, students had difficulty memorizing Avogadro's number. This is an important number to remember in order to perform calculations. Since they were having such a difficult time, I told them they could always call an avocado at 602-1023. It worked! From that moment forward, they knew it to be 6.02×10^{23}. Since that day, I've had students think of silly and absurd ways to help them recall challenging material. Given that humor fosters a culture of enjoyment in the classroom, it helps to build bridges between people by creating a culture of fun. We didn't always have to be serious because they were taking heavy-duty sciences.

Students witnessed whatever tickled my funny bone at any moment, and it didn't matter if I was laughing at myself or giggling with them. For example, after a heavy day of lectures, my tongue notoriously didn't want to work properly at the end of the day. My words tended to blend into absurd sentences. I made up for this with passionate and empowering body movements such as arms swinging and tiptoeing as I glided across the classroom explaining topics. It was like interpretive dance for science, something my seventh and eighth periods were privy to enjoy.

Hey, they laughed. I laughed. We laughed, and we are all healthier when we laugh.

Mindfulness Journey

This is not the packaged product that has been ruminated over in mainstream media and on social media platforms. This is truly having compassion for all other beings, which is difficult even for the most mindful Buddhists in our society. Mindfulness practice includes accepting yourself and others while being fully aware of the environment and acknowledging what is happening within the mind. It is the practice of learning to not be overly reactive or judgmental, which requires reassessment of thoughts and learning how to change thought patterns.

This is something I have been experimenting with on a personal basis and has brought more joy to my personal and work lives. At the time, I thought it would be fascinating to share this journey with my classes. With social media and negative news, unpleasant experiences seem to be attacking students' well-being, which is why I choose to help them daily. It worked, and they loved it!

Each day included a four-to-five-minute mindfulness session: Meditation Monday, Yoga Tuesday, Watchafeelin' Wednesday, Thankful Thursday, and Friendship Friday. Each day, we would spend a few minutes concentrating on wellness, whether that wellness was physical or mental.

According to the Centers for Disease Control website, in 2019, more than 36 percent of high school students felt sad or hopeless, and over 18 percent seriously considered suicide. As far as I am concerned, mental health disorders have turned into a public health crisis. I witnessed the issues with my students and was determined to give them a fighting chance with mindfulness tools.

As I said, this was a consciousness journey that seemed to help the students with their well-being. Whether they found a positive note they wrote in their pocket during a difficult class, a gratitude statement they shared, or they remembered to breathe before saying something they would regret to a classmate, the bulk of my students benefitted from this practice.

I modeled and demonstrated mental tools they could use to bring calmness to their minds, and they practiced this mindfulness with me. A few students said it helped them reset their thoughts during stressful moments, bringing a few minutes of peace during a troublesome situation. Just spending a few minutes each day made some of my students more resilient to setbacks by helping them increase their self-awareness and reduce their stress. In addition, it improved their focus and concentration in class. A win-win for everyone involved.

Safety and Refuge

This doesn't necessarily refer to safety, such as gun safety, fighting safety, or lab safety. This refers to feeling safe, whether physical, emotional, or psychological. If my students can be themselves, work toward achieving goals, and know it is okay to struggle in the classroom, then I have managed to create a safe place for students to learn.

Think of what makes you feel safe. Is it a warm blanket, a roaring fire in the fireplace, or the smell of clean laundry? Or is it more cerebral, such as feeling harmonious by being involved with people who embrace change and enjoy diverse perspectives, or is it knowing that an open-minded person is available to discuss personal matters?

I prided myself on providing a safe space for students to be themselves. Whether it be during class or after school, I have tried to be a dependable, safe space where students wanted to be and tended to gravitate. For example, as a sponsor of a student-led career organization, many students were willing to compete in various competitions. This differs from years past when they were unwilling to participate. They knew that before and after their respective competitions, I would be there cheering them on and showing them unconditional support.

During my evolution as a teacher, I discovered that my students learned they can feel comfortable not knowing the answer to a question. My students and I learned that we could all "fail forward" and learn from our mistakes. Each year, students would learn to feel good about trying to discover an answer and accept validation when they applied concepts.

It is equally important to have colleagues and teammates who are adaptable and willing to work towards the common good—our students. I feel like I have a shield of security when my team of teachers plans and implements strategic lessons that benefit the students. I much prefer being within a forest of other trees, all living harmoniously within an ecosystem, not feeling like a lone leaf dangling precariously on an isolated tree as it sways in the breeze. It is truly a joyous occasion when your team is a supportive, collaborative group.

Lab Coats, Paint, and Creative Problem Solving

You may be asking, "Doc, how does this work? How does a safe and mindful classroom form due to labs?" Aren't they just cookie-cutter worksheets with activities?" Nope!

Guided labs help students understand what they should be doing and instruct them as they learn new material. Hands-on assignments can be a variety of items such as colors, noodles, tape, colorful paper, cotton balls, yarn, or even just using the mouth to train the brain through connection-making. It can even include pantyhose and oatmeal. Yes, I used those two words in a sentence, and now I'm laughing at myself.

Integrating art into science is a marvelous combination in the classroom. It is more than using macaroni to demonstrate the skeleton's bones. It can include movement, music, visual representations, painting, dance, and poems. Anything that is fun and applies content at a deep level is the key. When I use this as an educational tool, I have always made it relevant to what they are learning, and I have never graded a student on their ability to do artwork. Ability and effort are different. There is clearly a difference between something hastily done right before class and something that took time and effort but shows little artistic ability.

Hey, I can barely draw a stick figure!

Problem-solving can occur in a multitude of forms: case studies, discussions, or even hands-on activities. Critical thinking involves identifying a problem, creating possible solutions, experimenting with potential solutions, and then deciding which solution is best. At that point, the remedy chosen is implemented, and the results are shared with others. In my case, some form of laboratory report is required. When I first started teaching, I required formal, typed lab reports. Over time, I modified the requirement to include artwork and other forms of visual representations.

An example is the pinto bean experiment I would assign to advanced biology students. They would receive ten pinto beans, a few paper towels, a resealable plastic bag, and a grading rubric. Their job was to use their imagination to test the best way to sprout pinto beans and continue that growth so that the plants would grow a few sets of leaves. This was all done at their homes. They had a few weeks to experiment and submit their laboratory report with proof of pinto bean growth. I was always amazed at the ingenuity and resourcefulness of my fourteen-year-old scientists. Some used different concentrations of coffee or soda. Some students used soil, and some did not. One student even grew bean plants on the ceiling fan in her bedroom. While her mother was not pleased with the outcome, I was delighted with her experimental design.

Allowing creativity and choice spurs the imagination and enhances a student's ability to grow as a learner. This was something that I learned during the many years of my career. I struggled to learn how to trust my students to solve problems on their own, with very little input from me. I learned to let go of typical teacher control and let the students "take the wheel" in their own process of learning.

Collaboration with Counterparts

Just what is a collaborative team? It is a group of people who endeavor toward a common goal. In education, that goal is student success. I've had some spectacular peers and colleagues throughout the years, some that aren't quite as amazing, and, of course, colleagues who refuse to be team members. It is wonderful to have a trusted team you can bounce ideas off of, problem-solve with, and split the workload with. I've had the opportunity to be part of an efficient and compassionate team of science teachers, and I miss working with each of them.

One of my fondest memories is from a suburban school that had an upgrade in the health science lab over the summer. We had extra funds to buy new supplies, so my partner, Jamie, and I worked diligently to find the best prices and items we could buy with the funds we were allotted. It required a great deal of time and effort, and it paid off when we started opening boxes. We were like two small girls opening a pile of birthday presents. One such box had a mannequin of a child in it wrapped in clear plastic, but the face was completely covered in white tissue and then covered in clear plastic. We both jumped in horror when we opened the box and laughed until our bellies ached. It was creepy and weird, and we couldn't stop laughing.

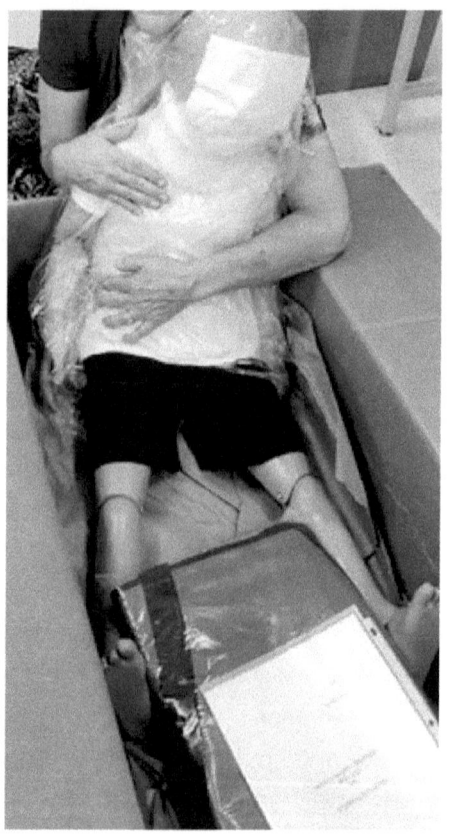

Jamie and I collaborated as friends and professionals. We shared ideas, solved problems, coordinated our time in that beautiful lab, and rewrote the curriculum during the summer together. When she retired, I made sure she had a wonderful celebration.

It is difficult when your peers and colleagues are negative and unwilling to work as a team. Yes, I've also experienced that aspect of noncollaboration. When the colleagues you see day-to-day are pessimistic and unwilling to work together to help students achieve success, it truly makes each day challenging. A supportive atmosphere can be crashed into darkness and misery quickly with adversarial peers.

Since I've been a singleton for much of my career, I've had very few teachers I could effectively innovate with in the past. When I have had the opportunity to include diverse perspectives and adapt to changing school conditions as a team, I've jumped at the opportunity. Whether it is figuring out new technology, training a team of middle school teachers how high school covers genetics in biology, or helping with the interview process to replace a teacher in my department, I have always lent a helping hand—joyously.

School Administrative Stewardship

Good administration can raise you to a higher level of educator effectiveness, emboldening a teacher to try new moves and attempt to reach intangible objectives. Reasonable administration can also call your bluff when you are too immersed in your perceived abilities, but in a professional and kind manner with convincing direction.

Bad administration can cause you to feel ineffective, unimportant, and easily replaceable. Faculty should be supported, and when you must deal with an ineffective and uncaring administrator, it can destroy your sense of well-being and effectiveness. This is unacceptable on all levels.

The administration at both the campus and district levels has quite a bit of balancing with a limited budget, and I empathize with the circumstances they must deal with daily. However, I think some requirements for effective administration are nonnegotiable.

Administration should be held accountable for their decisions and actions. It doesn't matter if the issue involves decorating the hallways for homecoming, if students are allowed to eat outside during lunch, or if someone should have their contract non-renewed. Administration should train their teachers and staff with useful professional development, such as allowing time for teachers to create lesson plans together, learn new technology skills, or review textbooks being considered for adoption. In addition, the administration should openly communicate with all faculty in a professional and transparent fashion. Whether in person or through email, we all deserve to be treated honestly as the professionals we are.

As an educator in the public school system, I serve all students and am proud to know I've impacted many. I have watched some students grow from timid wallflowers to leadership lilies over four years in and outside the classroom. Many of these students have stayed in contact through social media. As one enthusiastic student commented on Facebook, "Your dedication, passion, and enthusiasm pushed me every day, and it's not one moment that I can describe, but you being there and inspiring me in so many different aspects over four years that made it so memorable."

I hope newer teachers stick around long enough to feel they have contributed to student success. Unfortunately, I have seen many leave the classroom despite the passion they feel for the job due to inadequate administration. How is this acceptable?

"Education is the most powerful weapon which you can use to change the world."

~ Nelson Mandela

Chapter 4

Be Worthy of Trust

Years ago, I had a department chairperson who was dedicated, honest, and kind. Actually, I had two at the same time because I was technically in two departments due to the classes I taught. Both amazing women displayed those personality traits, and I still love them for their support. During the trials and tribulations associated with the garden I wrote of in Chapter 2, they supported me each step of the way. One of these ladies wrote a letter to the school superintendent about how the garden played a role in her photography curriculum, and the other showed up with shovels and pots in hand to help remove the garden on that cold, blustery, wintry day.

As leaders, they would always take the time to answer questions, help with budgetary issues, and address concerns. I trusted them as department chairpersons, and I still trust them as friends.

Did you have a teacher you could trust when you were in school? Why did you trust that teacher? What did they do to ensure the trust you felt? How about one you didn't trust? Why did you find that person unworthy of trust? Did it affect the way you viewed the subject matter you were studying in their class? Did you feel compelled to succeed in that class?

I've had a wide variety of different types of humans in my room. Different sizes, different colors, different belief systems with different types of home life, and I've learned that students display their trust in your ability as a teacher and a person in different ways. I had a boy named Sanjay who will forever be favorably burned into my memory, as he showed his trust differently than any student I had encountered during my years of teaching. Sanjay would dash into my room. "Hey Doc, what's up? What are we doing today?" He did this every day between classes, always on his way to another classroom. My usual response involved sarcasm and some form of interpretive dance. I raised an eyebrow, dramatically swung my arm, and pointed at the interactive screen at the front of the classroom. I then circled my arm toward the side of the room where I had placed whiteboard strips. On these strips, I would write daily objectives, student questions, learning outcomes, and important dates. Did I mention that sarcasm and interpretive dance are my secondary languages?

Sanjay always smiled broadly and said, "Yeah, you always know what's up, Doc." He would then saunter around the room, fingers grazing the tabletops, and leave saying, "See you later, Doc." I wondered about that boy. He was infuriating and chaotic, and it drove me bonkers, but I adored him. When he didn't pass through my classroom between classes, I knew something was wrong; he'd be upset. On those days, I would ask him, "What's up?" before class started, and he usually explained, in detail, ad nauseam. It's funny how I became his safe place to vent.

That's also part of the undefined aspects of a teacher's job. Teachers have become untrained, part-time, unpaid social workers and therapists. Some days, it bolstered me as well as the kid. Other days, I realized I couldn't help, and all I could do was listen. As I said before, my classroom was a safe place. On other days, I have called in the big dogs with appropriate qualifications and expertise who enjoyed a higher pay grade. Who are these awesome people? They are the unappreciated counselors who don't have time to counsel. Fortunately, serious situations were few and far between in my classroom.

Why do I bring this up in this chapter about trust? I'm sure you've heard that classroom expectations and the mood are based on the first-day interactions, and I agree that fundamental rules should be solidly laid out—as a foundation. But a safe classroom's true heart and soul are built on trust.

Yes, trust isn't just any five-letter word.

Let's discuss the word trust. Trust can be defined as dependence on something future or contingent, hope. Just what is the definition of hope? It is longing for something to occur, to nurture a wish with expectation. All I've ever wanted for my students is to trust, have hope, and use what they have learned to better their community and lives in some way. How did I help them in this endeavor every day?

Lesson Plans

Lesson plans. Really? Yes, I'm serious. Lesson plans really do represent something in the future, perhaps something to be anticipated. I must admit that lesson plans are plans and can be deviated from as needed. Student behavior and attitude hinge on class activities being dependable and something to look forward to. It is a kind of reward for hard work and persistence, as students should work toward passing grades. They should also uphold a wish to learn more. This leads to lifelong learning.

Lesson plans would lead to excited anticipation of an upcoming event. I would post lesson plans for each unit, allowing the students to know what would happen during the next few weeks. Each spring, my environmental science students would ask when we would be doing the ecosystem project. It was a project that always garnered interest from a variety of students, not just my own. I would tell them to keep an eye on the lesson plans. As soon as I posted the project, many students started planning how to build it well before the start date. It never failed. A few students would show up with betta fish, bottles, and building materials before I had a chance to discuss the project with each class.

How do I describe this project? Hum... Three bottles were cut and stacked on top of each other to create a tower. The bottom was a little water ecosystem with fish, gravel, water plants, and snails. The second layer was a decomposition chamber with a piece of fruit, soil, leaves, and at least one earthworm. The top layer was the terrestrial layer, with a bean plant and a worm in the dirt. In my first year with this project, we kept crickets in the top layer. After a while, they would smell and eat each other despite the amount of food available. I stopped doing that part of the project after the first year. It was nasty.

They built it, kept everything alive, and monitored each environment, including the fish's water. Theoretically, the fish should be able to live off what falls from the decomposition chamber, but I had the kids feed the fish. Student groups would have to determine the amount of water, how often testing should have occurred, and all additional analyses associated with this project. Some of my students had their fish for years after the project's conclusion. I was surprised how many shared this with me on social media, filling my heart with joy. One previous student's son has a betta fish in celebration of the fun she had with the project in my class!

This activity lasted between six and eight weeks. Occasionally, the fish would die, and we would have funerals for them. Sometimes, the plants would grow fast and produce beans, and the kids would snack on them. Sometimes, everything would go sour and smell horrible, and sometimes, it would grow into a nearly self-sustaining ecosystem. This was all scheduled in my lesson plans. A contract with the students led to a reward they hoped to receive, thus trust in the teacher and themselves. In addition, there were few surprises regarding graded materials, such as quizzes and tests, since everything was always listed and linked.

Earlier, I asked if you could spend time with a teacher from your school years, why would you spend time with them? Did you trust them? Were they the type of person who would be honest, truthful, and follow through with what they said? Spend some time rolling that around your skull.

With that being said, this is how every class began. All were welcomed with a smile. Do I always hang out at the door and shake their hands as they enter? Do you remember COVID-19? Nope, nope, and triple-nope on handshakes, but they were always given a genuine smile. In addition, I'm a science teacher, so I would clean, set up, reorganize, and provide quick reminders to students as they would run into my room. Shall I remind you of Sanjay?

After welcoming the kiddos, I pointed out the meme on my interactive board as I talked about the agenda for the day, objectives, and a quick "You should know [blah blah blah] by the end of class."

Now, I know that may seem a bit boring, but I can assure you that my sense of humor is, well, interesting. The memes were usually about the content we were covering, or at least something I thought was ridiculously funny when I created the slide show.

So, how does this show trust? My students trusted and hoped I would crack a joke, laugh at myself, or make a fuss as I welcomed them to class. They also trusted that I would be fair and that I would respect them as dynamic, imaginative, and intelligent young adults.

They also knew to put away any distractions that would not be used in class that day. Phones, computers, iPads, and all technology were to be put away. I preferred for them to color or doodle while I lectured or reviewed material. Seriously, am I the only one who seems to notice that technology is sucking the life out of our kids? One day, I predict we will read studies on this era and the long-lasting impacts little screens have on the brain.

Don't get me wrong, many screen-facing zombies groaned when I reminded them how many phones hadn't been put away. With a serious expression, I reminded them that their phone friends needed to rest and recharge at the phone station. Regularly, several would hide those damned things and think I didn't notice. Who looks down in their lap and smiles during a science class? If it wasn't a phone, I didn't want to know what they were smiling at.

Back to trust.

I looked at my lesson plans as a contract with my pupils. I fulfilled my contract to the best of my ability, and as part of that contract, they had the tools to follow through on their end. With an online learning management system, I posted the lesson plans with all content linked as a live document. They trusted that I would keep them apprised of current activities and changes—everything they could possibly need to be successful was posted. I can't take credit for having linked lesson plans; a colleague shared this idea with me, and I have used it ever since. We will talk about Sebastian later.

Back in the day, when I first started teaching, we did not have readily available online access. Heck, our computers barely worked properly last century. I still had the same expectations and guidelines. Everything they needed was clearly stated on the chalkboard. It was easily accessible if the student would take the time to write down assignments in a notebook or calendar each day. Yes, we used chalkboards back then.

Back to today.

How did they see this material if I didn't allow technology? They could use their computers when I gave permission. That way, they could complete meaningful assignments that had goals and expectations associated with them. They trusted that the work that I gave was not "busy work." It wasn't a waste of time or a loss of brain cells and neurotransmitters due to misuse. Simply put, they trusted me.

In my eyes, lesson planning showed them that you cared about how you planned your assignments so that they were successful. My students knew that I was willing to spend time and energy on their future, their passing, and their receiving credit. They knew I had a stake in their future and faith in their abilities.

But what if I needed to go back and reteach or dream of a cool activity while I was in the shower? I didn't get enough sleep during the school year, so yes, I dreamed in the shower. Or maybe I read of an activity that would be perfect that next day as a follow-up to a learning experience. I deviated from the lesson plans and told the kids I'd update them as soon as possible. I would even write a note on the lesson plans and highlight the note to let them know that there would be updates.

Just how did the students use the lesson plans to their advantage? A brown-headed, lively tenth grader by the name of Lily struggled in chemistry and continued in my class as an eleventh grader in environmental science. She would tell me how much she appreciated my lesson plans and updates because she felt she was doing something right by looking up the lesson plans before asking me. She often complained that many teachers made her feel inadequate and small when she asked about due dates or assignments. Lily undeniably felt I trusted her and her peers by empowering them with the necessary tools. Updated, accurate, and predictable lesson plans—that's what was needed. Very few curricular surprises occurred in my classroom.

Students need to trust their teachers, people who are role models and gatekeepers to their future. A teacher must be even-keeled, moderate in temperament, and wildly excited in their passion for the classroom.

How did I do this every day? I didn't. If you know how to do this every day, please reach out to me. I tried my best every day, but sometimes . . . well, I'm human.

Keep in mind that I did my best to be kind, empathetic, and compassionate, but as you know, perfection is not always attained. Some kids just push your buttons, and dealing with the insolence has become more difficult over the years. I've had plenty of those. All I had been able to do with difficult students was try to form a relationship through trust and humor. If that didn't work, I had to move on but still continued to use encouragement and positivity. They usually came around and became less difficult.

Trust. You can't force it, just like you can't make a horse drink water even though you have led them to the trough. I advertised my availability, and when they were ready to reach out, I was truly accessible.

Josh, a junior taking law enforcement classes at my campus, was one of these difficult students. At the beginning of the school year, he would look over his paper at me, slightly sneering. Around January, he warmed up and apologized for being obnoxious to me during class. Josh had been traumatized in previous science classes and felt he was unable to understand science concepts. He eventually stated that I made the class interesting and that "There were never any surprises since expectations were clear-cut," and he felt that I was approachable. He even admitted that he bypassed his dislike of science and loved it due to my class. He's now a forensic scientist, and I feel like a proud mama bear!

Let's go back to a variation of the questions from earlier. Did you have moments where you didn't feel safe or allowed to be yourself around adults? I bring this up because trust is vitally important between teachers and administrators. If an administrator is trustworthy and helpful, you feel supported and protected within the school walls. If your administrator is untrustworthy, you feel quite vulnerable, even as a failure, despite your best efforts.

Think of someone you don't trust and why you don't trust that person. Now imagine that person being your superior at work. Wow, it brings butterflies to my stomach.

At one point, I had an administrator falsify evaluations because she rarely visited my classroom. The praise was usually aboveboard, so I didn't argue. During one of the many school years that she was my supervisor, I needed assistance with a student who thought it was okay to call me inappropriate cuss words. I needed her to step in and issue consequences. What was I told? It was explained that I was required to bargain with this student on my own; if I couldn't handle it, I should consider moving to a smaller school district. I would receive no support from her because she was too busy.

Other times, I've had supervisors who didn't return phone calls or emails and then demanded that I respond in the evenings via text. That has happened a few times during my teaching career. When teachers reach out for help with a student, it needs to happen during the school day, not after hours. At one school, I was admonished openly in front of a classroom for reaching out to a different administrator because my supervisor was not available. This isn't just disturbing for the student who is struggling; it is disquieting for the entire class. Needless to say, the expectations were unbelievable when haggling with this insufficiently callous supervisor.

Just what qualities does someone possess that make them worthy of trust? It is so much more than daily routines and so much more than lesson plans. Someone who is trustworthy is a person who follows through with their word and deed. Someone who is trustworthy pays attention to what you have to say and implements that input. Someone who is trustworthy applies their knowledge and skills to the best of their ability.

In the world of teaching, it is someone who grades fairly and in a timely manner. It is an educator who accepts criticism of test questions and grades since they are aware that they are fallible. Now, I did not allow students to lead me down a rabbit hole when grades were discussed, but I did allow them to write down their questions so I could consider the argument when I was not distracted. This built trust with students because I would not waste their valuable time with such meandering tactics students tend to apply. This reminds me of Georgia.

Georgia was an ambitious, determined, and gregarious senior who was second in her graduating class. She decided to aggressively argue with me about a question on a test. I remember clearly, "But Doc, I thought the question asked something else, and that's why I answered the way I did." I explained that she needed to write it down so I could consider her words. Her response was emotional: "Why can't you just give me a break?" I stood my ground and repeated the rules I wanted her to follow about grade questions. She angrily stared at me but remained quiet. Georgia showed her determination to change my mind and interrupted a class later in the day to discuss the same test question. After a few minutes, I had her meet me in the hallway to discuss fairness and respect. I then reiterated the rules and sent her back to class. The next day, she apologized and handed me an extensive document arguing her point. Georgia worked exceptionally hard to gain credit for that test question!

Many of my colleagues would have turned Georgia away and not considered her request, but I didn't. If she wanted credit, she had to abide by the rules, just as everyone else was required to do. At her graduation, she hugged me and thanked me for that specific lesson. She knew that she tended to be impulsive and obsessive at times. I hugged her back and told her that she would do great things in the future. She's now in medical school. Another proud mama bear moment!

Ahhh, trust. As I said before, it isn't just any five-letter word. For a teacher, it includes expectations, an ear for listening, a heart for sharing, an ability to plan, an eye aware of student needs, empathy, and a mouth for laughter. Just what is trust to you? To my students and me, it is a genuine personality that is honest, fair, compassionate, and inclusive. This should also apply to the administration of a school environment, which leads to positive morale for faculty and staff.

"Trust is the glue of life. It's the most essential ingredient in effective communication. It's the foundational principle that holds all relationships."

~ Stephen Covey

Chapter 5

Be a Genuine Person

When I started teaching in the late 1990s, I had been advised not to become sociable with students for the first month. I was told not to smile, and it was my job to "put them in their place." Since I was new to the profession, I followed that advice for most of the first day and was miserable. The second day was much more memorable because I smiled and had fun with the kids. I'm not an inflexible, narrow-minded person, and I find joy in connecting with other people, especially my students. My first day on the job was not satisfactory due to terrible advice.

To develop relationships with students, I've relied on my ability to teach, relay information, and compel them to apply that knowledge. As they grew to know me through the school year, students realized I was an honest, knowledgeable, ridiculously fair, and reliable teacher. They knew in their hearts that I was the kind of teacher who would reach into their hearts and inspire them to be inquisitive and develop their passions, whatever those passions might be. Once they realized that I had a clear vision and a strong purpose, they learned how to respond to each other with kindness as they modeled my behavior. It didn't take long for pupils to realize that it was safe to struggle with content and that it was okay to be imperfect. They saw that I was a genuine person without alternative aspirations. I had their backs. This was an incredibly eye-opening experience for most of them because they were not accustomed to being treated fairly by a trustworthy, genuine person: a teacher who could also be a protective mama bear.

This reminds me of Andy, a fresh-faced ninth grader with dark hair and dark eyes, in an advanced biology class I once taught. He was timid, quiet, and reserved toward me during much of his first year of high school, although I recognized his exploratory questions. He also tended to lead his cohort of peers in lively discussions and laboratory activities. Around November, he asked to speak with me about his future and wanted my input. I had him explain his interests and where he could see himself in five, ten, and fifteen years. Andy aspired to be a political figure who played a role in medicine to administer proper health care to all the people of our world. I stated that this was a wonderfully grand goal and accomplishable if he had a strong foundation in biology so he could take it to the next level in further classes and studies. After this meeting, he was more open to me in class. He realized that the rigor and significance of my class would be beneficial to his future, and I made sure to turn his excitement and passion for the subject into a class project of sorts.

Ninth graders were usually rotated in small groups throughout the school year. I made sure that each student would be rotated to work with Andy so they could problem-solve together. Examples included complex genetic problems, application during dissections, and the design of environmental habitats for artfully self-created animals and plants. These were all examples of the labs and hands-on activities you would witness if you entered my wild realm of controlled chaos.

You may be thinking this woman was playing favorites with this child. No, I saw Andy's potential in class and made use of it to raise the awareness of other students, ones who didn't have the same commitment to their education. It worked!

During this ongoing school year, COVID-19 arrived on our doorstep—in March of 2020.

We were isolated, living behind screens and barriers from each other. I knew this would be very difficult for all of us, and I had grown perpetually concerned for all my students, including Andy. Despite my concerns, he became a beacon of light as a student who continued to excel. He met virtually with the local Medical Reserve Corps, received training online, and began to head a group of peers who worked to help the community in various ways. This group of incredibly selfless individuals regularly met online and committed themselves to helping the community. Eventually, they created interactive blankets for Alzheimer's patients, built and grew a small culinary garden at school, and retrieved materials to create first aid kits for the visually impaired. Andy had taken the skills learned in class to bring people together and guided them to do wholesome activities for themselves and the community.

Andy continued this behavior in his other classes as his self-esteem grew, and he found his true calling as a leader and future medical doctor. It has been a few years since he graduated, and he still stays in regular touch with what he is learning and how he is doing in college. I recently received an Amazon gift card from him as a holiday gift, which I promptly spent on printer ink. His gift of kindness made me cry with joy. He and his companions will forever change the world!

Another aspect of being genuine is being aware of what is going on with each student, even when there are over twenty-five students in a class. Random recognition of little things, such as when a student has lost interest in a topic, there will be a sagging of the shoulders, or a frustrated student may appear to participate but not really do the assignments, or even worse, refuse to participate. How about that girl who is angry with her significant other, the boy with an angry mother, or the child who had to work eight hours after school to keep his family from being evicted from their apartment?

I made it a point to recognize issues, although I couldn't reach out to every student each day. There simply aren't enough minutes in a school day, but I can play a role in guiding them back to the lesson after a pat on the back or supplying a knowing look in their direction. Yes, even with the most difficult of students.

Carla was a student in a specialized environmental studies program. A blonde girl with inquisitive eyes and a sharp tongue, she was not interested in solving problems that didn't benefit her directly. Her chatty lab partner was more interested, but not by much. Carla and her friend were not strong juniors, and they knew this specialty class was not based on tests and quizzes but on projects and problem-solving. As far as they were concerned, this class was an easy A.

This specialized environmental science class analyzed local ecological problems, created prototypes, and prepared grants to receive funds to build these prototypes and use those creations to benefit the environment in some way. To sum it up, the class was based on problem-solving techniques that guided students to directly impact their community through ecological stewardship.

After much poking and prodding on my part, I discovered that both girls enjoyed spending time at a local lake and were disgusted with the green goo that had been growing at their favorite spot. I had them read a few articles about natural water filtration processes, which piqued their interest. The pair was determined to find an approach to mitigate the problem. "Doc, do you know what eutrophication is? The nasty green slime is there because people are stupid. They put too much fertilizer out, and those nutrients stimulate the algae to grow! Then that algae dies and uses up the oxygen in the water when they decompose! That is so wrong! How do we fix it?"

These two came up with a battle plan. The first plan was to start an educational campaign to change their community's behavior. They soon realized that it is difficult to change people's behavior.

They put the campaign on hold and decided to design a water filtration prototype. Soon, they were busy writing a proposal for grant funds and purchasing supplies. After a few weeks of blood, sweat, and tears, they created a mini ecosystem in a plastic pool at the back of the classroom lab. In this controlled environment, they created an issue with eutrophication and then added water plants and a bubbler to supply oxygen. These two young ladies monitored the water through testing and observation. After a few more weeks, water testing showed it was working, and they were thrilled!

Our Future Farmers of America barn was about one mile down the road, and there were regular issues with algae in the creek behind the barn. After establishing a working prototype, they had hoped to build their innovation behind the barn to help with the algae growth and make the area more pleasant for the local flora and fauna—for people, too.

Do you remember the story about the garden in Chapter 2? The head administration decided not to be open to the idea, and no, they didn't have the opportunity to build their creation. Argh. How cool would that have been?

Even though they didn't have the opportunity to build their concept in the community, they did have the chance to showcase it at City Hall in front of stakeholders such as businesspeople, educators, political figures, and peers. The highlight of the evening was when the mayor of our city stopped by to ask questions about their project. They were so giddy with excitement that I thought they had seen a musical pop star! Yes, this is another one of the memorable moments that students mentioned as fond memories. After numerous years, this venue was the most memorable for these two girls in my classroom, although technically, it was not in the classroom.

How is this a story about being genuine and its importance in the classroom? I sincerely believed they could create something that would have an impact. I championed their cause, let them use critical thinking skills to solve a problem, and guess what? They built it!

Everyone needs to have genuineness in their lives. Children, teens, adults, older people, we all need to have someone who has unconditional faith in our abilities. The perceived belief in ourselves due to the outside graciousness of others keeps us going. How is this any different in a school?

Back to a variation of a question asked earlier. What were some of the personality traits of a teacher that helped you feel empowered to learn? Did you trust them? Were they genuine? How about humor—did they help you find humor in your life? Apparently, that is one of my never-ending teacher qualities, according to previous and current students. That makes me want to laugh out loud!

At the start of this chapter, I explained how I tried not to smile or show kindness toward my students at the start of the school year. Since that time, I have trained myself to be more compassionate, a skill that can be broadened with practice. This has made me more mindful and, thus, more genuine in my dealings with people, including my students.

During a particular school year, when I had three large science classes and two very active clubs, I met Christine as a student in my chemistry class. She was introverted among her peers, but not with me. She struggled in my class due to a learning disability and took her educational struggles in stride; therefore, she stayed after school for tutorials on a regular basis. Our relationship developed into a mentor/student partnership as the days passed. As I got to know her, I discovered she was industrious, curious, and quick-witted. We would pass jokes back and forth as I helped her with her lessons. It was great fun. Outside of sharing jokes, I assisted her with her study skills. As a result of our connection, she decided to take advanced placement environmental science and excelled in the class, getting a five on the advanced placement exam at the end of the school year and receiving college credit for the course. That's no small feat!

Christine then enrolled in my specialized environmental science class, which involved critical thinking, problem-solving, and environmental stewardship. She found her passion and was eventually accepted into an honors college program at a university. She is now in the United Kingdom working as an engineer at an innovative solar power company, helping to develop renewable energy sources.

Christine and I have stayed in touch throughout the years. One day, she emailed me with a thank you and an explanation for the thanks. She stated that I empowered her to learn, that I "never gave up on her," and that my "authentic nature toward her success played a huge role in her determination and drive to help humanity." I read her words through tears of joy. Yes, another proud mama bear moment.

I haven't mentioned administration personnel in this chapter, except in passing. As I've said before, I've had real, genuine administrators as supervisors, and I've had distrustful supervisors. That's all I'm going to say about that at this point. The stories in this chapter are positive and heartwarming, so let's just enjoy that aspect. In later chapters, we'll return to the pros and cons of administration techniques and how that affects teachers who are on the edge of leaving the profession.

"When educating the minds of our youth, we must not forget to educate their hearts."

~ Dalai Lama

Chapter 6

Humor is Healthy

Humor is like the bone, humorous—the not-so-funny bone. I know you, dear reader, may not think that makes sense, but I can guarantee my students get it. They know my sense of humor is way out in left field, full of sarcasm and attempted dramatizations.

Just what is humor? The humor I'm referring to is not telling jokes, rehearsed comedy skits, or anything I plan in my classroom. Between you and me, my true sense of humor would make me a successful late-night comedian, but that is not appropriate for a high school teacher. It is usually off the cuff, even on my not-so-good days. I can't explain how I make strong student connections with humor, but I can give plenty of examples of humor and why I know it is a vital part of life, not just in my profession. Well, my current profession.

The kind of humor I'm referring to here includes simple chuckles, small smiles, and full-blown, deep, throaty guffaws. Humor is not taking yourself so seriously that you can't have fun. My classroom is serious, with high expectations and fun sprinkled like rainbows on a sunny day. For example, some words don't work with my tongue, but I can say "trichotillomania" easily. For instance, I cannot correctly say "sphygmomanometer" (blood pressure cuff). Since I have taught anatomy-based courses, I have had to use the scientific word periodically. Whenever I use this word, I usually drool a little. I know that's gross. When I ran across that word, I would try to say it, dramatically wipe at the dibble of drool, and have a student pronounce it for me. This always gets a chuckle, and there is a bit of shock value that is appreciated by all.

I don't mind showing students my imperfections; it is an indicator of my humanness.

As a bibliophile with books of many genres, I make sure to keep a few books about "how to teach" on the shelves of my home office. Before writing this chapter, I thumbed through them and didn't see any significant references to humor being a necessary part of a classroom. Making connections with students does fill plenty of pages, but not humor. I then did a quick Google search and found a multitude of websites that refer to the importance of humor in the classroom. An Edutopia article entitled "Using Humor in the Classroom" by Maurice Elias read, "It brings a sense of pleasure and appreciation and creates a common, positive emotional experience that the students share with each other and the teacher." Unfortunately, many of these sites suggest making fun of yourself to add humor in the classroom. I didn't intentionally make fun of myself daily. I laughed at my mistakes and moved on. This allowed the kids to laugh at themselves, permitting the release of positive chemicals in the brain, such as oxytocin and dopamine. These chemicals help elevate mood, provide a feeling of safety, and allow trust to grow. This brought a sense of connection and a safe place to make mistakes.

How did humor play a role in my classroom? It created a place my students wanted to be.

Lamar was a 6'5" football player who spent weekends chasing a ball across a field and sacking the other team. I don't know much about football, but Lamar loved to share his weekend escapades with me each Monday. One day, he was animatedly conveying some type of move he had made on the field. While speaking, he began jabbing his finger into a hole in the lab science workbench. This opening functions to hold chemistry materials during labs. Since this was a new lab, I was still awaiting many supplies, including the poles for the gaps in the tables. As he spoke, I became more aware of the depth of his finger in the table, and I warned him to stop so his finger would not become stuck. As he stated, "Nah, my finger won't get stuck," guess what happened?

No, you don't have to guess. I'll tell you.

His finger was jammed up to the top knuckle in the hole, and he could not retrieve it no matter how hard he tried. I became frantic and tried to pull his finger out myself, to no avail. I then grabbed the dish soap and some lotion and sent a student to get the school nurse. Lamar was trying to hide his emotions, but he was becoming increasingly alarmed when one of his friends said they would have to cut off his finger or call the Fire Department to bring the jaws of life. This was not the time for joking, but it alleviated some of the tension.

About the time the nurse ran into the room, we had managed to pull his finger out of the lab station. The whole class stood there looking at his finger with great relief, asking if it hurt and offering to get him some ice. He then left the room with the nurse. At that school, protocol dictated that the nurse assess any potential injury and contact the parents.

I'm not telling you this story because it is funny that he had his finger stuck in the table. I'm telling you this because of what happened in the nurse's office and after he returned to class.

Lamar returned about twenty minutes later; somewhat abashed and definitely embarrassed. Everyone laughed and clapped when he entered the classroom, yelling, "Bravo." At this point, Lamar sat down and told us about what happened in the nurse's office. When the nurse called his mother to tell her about the incident, she was having a manicure with her sisters and his aunts. The manicurist had put the call on speaker, and the entire nail salon heard about his escapade. This sparked immediate laughter and taunting by his family since he tended to get into "tight situations." While this may have upset some people, this entire episode was hilarious to him. And honestly, to everyone in the nail salon and my classroom, it was wonderful to end this potentially serious situation with humor.

Humor heals, laughter rejuvenates, and I am grateful that I didn't have to call the authorities to bring the Jaws of Life.

Our lives are stressful, and we are always "on the go" with technology leading us by the nose. Laughter and humor are ways to reconnect with our humanness. Laughter is contagious, a healing infection that can ease stress and plight. Humor keeps the kids motivated and engaged, even with difficult subjects. More than once, I've acted like I was going to bash my head into the board, especially when I taught chemistry. Their frustration always turned into laughter, and that is important because humor can be a tool to ease irritation. It didn't matter what needed to be cured. Humor is healthy, and laughter can make us forget the anxiety and angst we deal with daily. This is no different for students, colleagues, and administration.

I have already mentioned the memes, my sarcasm, and my endeavors at interpretive dance, so now it is time to introduce an Elf named Seymour Buttes with his new buddy, Hugh Jazz. I didn't discover Elf on the Shelf until well after my children were grown, so I felt compelled to buy one and have not regretted it. For years, they arrive on Halloween for a day, then reappear the day before Thanksgiving break. I look forward to about three weeks of Elf shenanigans for the rest of the year. Sometimes, the setups are detailed, sometimes simple. What truly matters is that the students race into the room each day to see what the elves are doing, and they either laugh or are grossed out.

One year, an upbeat, excitable freshman by the name of John reached out to touch the Elf, and one of my eighteen-year-old senior girls screamed, "Don't touch him; he will lose his magic." She was serious, and poor John jumped about two feet into the air and may have wet his pants. I jumped, too; her scream was frightening, although the situation was hilarious.

Some days, the elves were simply taped to the board with instructions for the pupils to follow. On other days, the Elves were melting Frosty the Snowman, and on different days, they may be found upside down, held by the skeletons in my classroom. It was utterly dependent on inspiration from the day before. I even developed a social media following with friends giving suggestions in October for the upcoming holiday season.

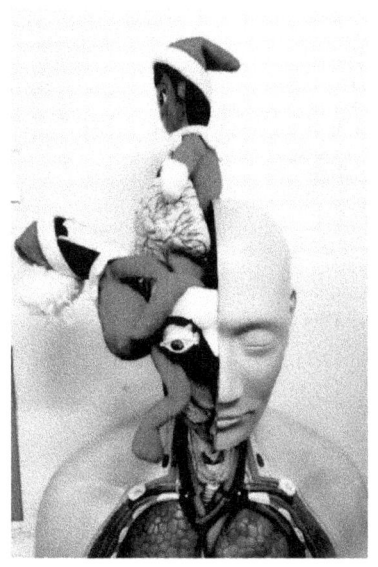

So why do I use humor in the classroom? One reason is that it is natural for me to smile and laugh. I had to smile on my first day as a teacher, it felt wrong not to smile. As Marlo Thomas said, "Laughter is important, not only because it makes us happy, but also because it has actual health benefits. And that's because laughter completely engages the body and releases the mind. It connects us to others, and that in itself has a healing effect."

As an educator, I've noticed that students enjoy my sense of humor unless they don't feel safe, so I've spent time asking students what makes them feel safe. I've had responses such as a warm sweater, warm water, hot tea, comforting friends, and the freedom to express emotions. How do we accept these items into our lives? Gratitude. Something that is minor in my world, such as a hot cup of coffee and a working computer as I type this book, may be substantial to someone else, especially when hot water being available for a comfortable shower is something that makes you feel safe.

According to Maslow's Hierarchy of Needs, students need physiological needs for survival, such as water, food, and shelter, as the first step in creating self-actualization. The second step is safety and security. Safety and security can be health, family, and the ability to be social and accepted. This leads to love and belonging. Friendship and a sense of connection can be established at this stage of development. All of this makes sense; we emit feel-good chemicals in our bodies as part of our nervous system when we feel safe, which leads to connection with others. How can a person play a role in their own learning, which leads to self-esteem and self-actualization, if they feel unsafe or under attack? They don't. Their bodies don't allow it, at least not easily.

If I can make my students feel safe to laugh, to appreciate and recognize gratitude, they can begin to feel joy.

That's how these cerebral concepts work in tandem, as I've learned through my own mindfulness journey. Thus, a feeling of safety, expressing gratitude, and experiencing laughter can lead to joy.

Laughter is how we share joy with others. It is how we develop companionship and connectedness between different types and styles of personalities, basically making connections with others. What should teachers do to get students to buy into the learning expectations and feel as if they belong? Make connections!

I openly show gratitude for little things and big things alike. And I laugh at myself a lot, and I mean a lot! Whether I'm called Dr. Evil during the late 1990s, trying to snap while slam poetry is being read as we cover some component of the curriculum, or explaining why I have a little green poop emoji on my desk, I laugh at myself regularly.

Outside of joy and gratitude, modeling proper ways to handle tough situations and bringing humor into the equation are vital. It is okay to make mistakes and have fun while doing something worthwhile. Why not demonstrate this each day? One of my graduates wrote on social media: "I loved joking around with you. You always made my day. Plus, I loved the way that you would get excited when you were proud of me for doing something right."

Her comment reminds me of a professional development session where I taught my nonscience colleagues a bit of chemistry and its interrelatedness with their career and technical courses. I had my peers perform a rainbow-colored chemistry experiment and then showed them how to do some basic chemistry equations that related to their courses. One of the teachers who was being educated that day kept talking about how much she hated math and that this was very stressful for her, but she was determined to figure out the equations I had demonstrated on the board. After a few minutes of hemming and hawing and excited heavy breathing, she expectantly handed me her paper. I quickly wrote 100 with smiley faces at the top. She was so excited about this she danced around the room like a circus clown. It was hilarious, and we ended our chemistry session laughing at her antics.

Humor is healthy and healing and is an indicator of safety, love, and belonging. It is an administration that would lip-sync lively holiday jingles as part of a school holiday video card as they donned proper holiday attire, such as ugly sweaters and elf costumes. It was always filled with laughter and humor. My favorite part of the video would always be the outtakes. The heads of the school laughed and had fun, making mistakes to entertain and wish the entire community a happy holiday. How wonderful it was!

There are boundaries to humor. It should never be offensive and shouldn't include anything that could be construed as cruel or unkind. I have had administrators make unkind "jokes" and thinly veiled disrespectful humor directed at me. At times, it has been racist, such as the time a student had a parent in jail due to attempted robbery. An administrator stated that it was "in the student's blood" to misbehave. Other times, it had been misogynistic. A colleague referred to women going to college for a "Mrs. Degree" and "Well, I guess you feel better about raising other people's children instead of your own since you aren't home taking care of them." How about the administrator who sprayed Lysol each day a schoolboy had to go to the office? "He's terrible and smells bad. I'm going to buy him some deodorant." What about religious bias? "Those ragheads have to put up with Christmas decorations because we are Christian in this country. Don't you agree, Doc?"

This has been a regular issue at each school I've been a part of, not just one administrator or peer making these statements in jest. I can visualize each face at different schools as I type this. I guess they thought I would appreciate their comments and jokes.

Nope, I did not.

How does a trustworthy, genuine, and humorous teacher interact with their students every day? I consciously model mindful behavior thrown in with interpretive dance and an attempt at tai chi and yoga. Let's see how that works as part of a mindfulness journey I am taking with my students.

"Laughter heals all wounds, and that's one thing that everybody shares. No matter what you're going through, it makes you forget about your problems. I think the world should keep laughing."

~ Kevin Hart

Chapter 7

Mindfulness Journey

I would stand in my classroom, looking at the empty desks before school started, chanting multiple times, "Thought . . . Word . . . Deed . . . Thought . . . Word . . . Deed . . ." Then I would fill my lungs to the count of four, hold for two, breathe out counting four, three, two, one, and hold my air for another count of two. This would continue for a few minutes until I felt grounded and ready to be a productive member of the faculty at my school and, thus, in society.

This is how I started my days on some occasions. Not every day, but on occasion. Regretfully, there are days when I have had to begin each class in this manner. I say the words in my head and don't count out loud as students enter the room. Some mindfully aware individuals noticed what I was doing and nodded a knowing acknowledgment. Others just burst into the room loudly, rambunctiously, ready to learn.

Most days in the years past, I didn't have to start the day this way, but more and more is required for my mental health—much more than I care to admit. Since the struggle has been real over the past few years, I've been on a journey to learn about mindfulness and how it can help me and my students.

What is mindfulness? Oh, my goodness, it is so much. It is most certainly not something you can buy in bulk at your local box store. Imagine how lucrative it would be to bottle it up and sell the real thing!

Mindfulness can be difficult; it is an ongoing daily process of looking within yourself and outside yourself. It is an aspiration to become a better person by being aware of the love, light, and energy of others, and it is of utmost importance when you are in service to others. Additionally, it has wonderful health benefits and brings a sense of safety to a classroom. How did I do that? Consciously, carefully, deliberately, and thoughtfully.

Stay with me for a few paragraphs as I explain something you may think is way the hell out there.

I firmly believe that your thoughts, words, and deeds all go hand in hand. Whatever your thoughts are, this will transform into a form of energy that can be favorable.

Watch out! Here comes the science teacher, and I feel compelled to explain what that means. Energy is neither created nor destroyed. It can transform. Think of a ball at the top of a hill. When the ball is at the top of the hill, it has the potential to roll down that hill. That's called potential energy. Once it begins to roll down the hill, it converts that potential energy into kinetic energy as it moves and picks up speed. That is the energy of movement, which can also be converted to thermal energy—heat.

Everyone has the capability of using the energy of their thoughts to create words, which can take the form of energy as you perform the deeds. Deeds are the acts, the actual activities because of the words and thoughts. Basically, it is what is done or accomplished.

Let's say I think about doing the dishes. I tell my husband I am going to do the dishes, and then I convert that energy into kinetic energy by doing the dishes. This short explanation is simplistic but accurate. We all do this every day. The difference is that I make it a point to intentionally create positive thoughts that can be transferred eventually into positive deeds. This is one of my forms of mindfulness.

Negative thoughts can turn into negative deeds, small or large. I could hurt someone's feelings or say something inappropriate. I want my deeds to feed my students' souls, not eat away at their being.

Unfortunately, in my line of work, there are bullies dressed as teachers who do not understand that we feed our students with our actions. For example, I have encountered situations with colleagues and future graduates that don't make sense to me. A fellow teacher harassed students to tears, making each of them feel that the harassment was their fault. Why would someone be in education and beat the individuality out of those who are growing into themselves? This person unjustly verbally attacked them when they were down, then filed falsified write-ups to continue to agitate these young men and young women. This is an example of someone who destroys our future, not uplifts and protects it.

Where was the administration on this issue? Despite complaints from students and me, administrators "talked" to this teacher as they performed an investigation. In the meantime, the attacked pupils struggled to stay afloat without parental backup due to a lack of the ability to speak English properly. More than one colleague has behaved this way toward students during my years in education, and it is disturbing.

I feel my heart breaking just thinking about this situation. Once again, where was leadership? What were they doing about this unhospitable behavior? I can tell you from experience that various administration officials were waiting for the pupils to graduate, hoping that "a good talking to" the bully would do the job. This would never be tolerated in the corporate world. Why do children have to tolerate it in the educational system?

Until the last few years, my husband thought all teachers were like me: forgiving and compassionate. Now, he understands the concern many people have about public education and the struggles I've dealt with. He also understands the importance I place on meditation, mindfulness, and the time I spend in reflection when I awake each morning.

Yes, it has been a struggle—a daily struggle. But I am still conscientious of being mindful. I get up early, practice yoga and tai chi, meditate, and reflect while the world is still quiet. It is part of my daily routine, and I feel incomplete and have difficulty concentrating on thoughts, words, and deeds if I don't practice my mindfulness moments in the morning.

I am constantly monitoring my process as I strive to assemble those thoughts that are productive, assured, and less disagreeable. What's within you should be modeled for others, especially your students. This displays that I am worthy of trust; students know I work toward bettering myself. When I am intentionally praiseful and kind, others see and feel that. It is genuine and real, shows trust, provides a sense of safety, and is practicing mindfulness.

Regarding a classroom based on mindfulness, I demonstrate it each day with a quote on the board and a few minutes of practical mindfulness activities. How can this be utilized with students?

A young lady was quite upset about missing out on being in a specialized certification program at our school due to misinformation from a counselor two years earlier. She could only focus on that closed door, and couldn't get past the anger she felt. After a short discussion about her alternatives, I asked her, "What do you see when you stare at a closed door?" She didn't know how to answer, so I did it for her. "All you see is a closed door, a lost chance, an ill-fated opportunity. Why not look at the other possibilities and change your mindset about this situation?"

For a few minutes, she just looked through me as she thought about her situation. Later, she told me that she felt much better about her problem and that perhaps it was "meant to be."

This is teaching mindfulness. But what is the true purpose, and is there any scientific reasoning behind practicing mindfulness?

Mental health issues have become openly prevalent in our society, as I commented earlier in Chapter 3. It is estimated that over 800,000 people committed suicide in 2016, with an assumption of underreporting in many countries across the globe. If I can do something to prevent this from occurring to one of my students, I will find a way.

If you search online, you will see a multitude of websites dedicated to this subject for various age groups. There are websites with tips, tricks, medications, and how to find professional assistance. Since I've had underlying depression for most of my life, I empathize with the plight of my students with diagnosed and undiagnosed mental ailments. Being resilient to setbacks, seeing the positive over the negative, and turning off the nasty self-talk is challenging when your mind is at odds with the world around you.

In my search to achieve better mental and physical clarity, I noticed the word mindfulness several times and began to search for books I could study to include it in my coping toolbelt. It has not disappointed, and plenty of peer-reviewed medical journals have secured documentation that agrees with me. Examples include *Academic Medicine*, the *Journal of the Association of American Medical Colleges*, the *Journal of Mental Health Counseling*, *Brain, Behavior, and Immunity-Health*, and the *Journal of Consulting and Clinical Psychology*. All have documented studies that include the potential powerfulness of mindfulness practices.

For instance, immune system regulation and inflammatory factors function irregularly in those with mental health challenges such as anxiety and depression. Mindfulness activities such as guided meditation, yoga, and gratitude journaling have been shown to decrease the inflammatory biomarkers in the blood and have helped to balance abnormal blood chemistry. Along with decreasing major depressive episodes and anxiety issues, happy hormones and mood-elevating neurotransmitter levels increase with increased mindful activities.

How did I choose to use this information with my students? With over one hundred students each day, it isn't physically possible to have mindfulness discussions with each set of focused eyes, so I experiment with four to five minutes of specific mindfulness sessions each class period at the start of class.

On Mondays, I attempt a five-minute Meditation Monday session, which has evolved into a short, controlled breathing session with light visualization. Honestly, two minutes is usually the maximum amount of time the kids can remain still. Teenagers still don't know how to sit and naturally breathe; their bodies still wiggle like small children. Their brains are not fully developed, and some don't understand why we are doing these exercises despite the explanation. Some are really into these moments. Others, not so much after being forced to be sedentary for most of their day.

Despite the wiggling and awkwardness at the beginning of Meditation Mondays, you can feel an energy change among the students. They are calmer. They are more focused, and they are ready to learn. On a side note, I've had a few students tell me how this practice has helped them deal with stress in different classes. "They don't know what I'm doing to calm down—it's so cool." I had wondered if they had been practicing independently. I am filled with pride knowing some students are using the tools practiced in class to tame their minds.

Yoga Tuesday is a bit strenuous. We do yoga stretching and light tai chi with controlled breathing. We partially lunge and squat, but not as much as I would like due to my old knees. They stay in the isometric contraction stage for a few seconds, and we flow into the next pose. Teenagers are instructed to bend over, touch their toes, and slowly roll back up while controlling their breathing; they then side stretch and move on to leg muscle stretching. We end with clapping our hands, rubbing the palms together, and silly wiggling in place. The energy change is palpable. It is great fun, and I love that my students have improved as the year has progressed.

Wednesday is Watchafeelin' Wednesday. Students write on a small piece of scratch paper how they are feeling that day. I have them hold it dear to their heart if it is something good and positive and rip it up into tiny pieces if it doesn't serve them as they deserve to be served.

On one of the first Wednesdays of the year, one of my clever and witty juniors, named Rob, was so excited he ripped his paper up and was quite upset that he did so. He yelled, "Oh no, it was a good thing, and I've ruined it." I ran over to him with the tape dispenser and told him to fix it and not to worry. It would be better than ever if he kept a grateful state of mind. He has since reminded me of that day and smiles a big, goofy smile each time he enters class.

I really believe they are thinking whatever that good thought is, putting it into words by writing it, and the next stage is . . . deed. I sure hope someone did something good with the affirmation they created for themselves. Isn't that thought pretty awesome?

Thursday is Thankful Thursday. It is based on gratitude journaling but a miniature version. Students write something down on a small piece of paper that they are grateful for. If it is a person, I let them know how important it is to share it with that individual. I have had them think about whatever they are grateful for and put it into words. I sound like such a New Ager when I tell them to hold onto that absolute thought and hold it close to their hearts because gratitude equals joy. Joy is what we all strive to achieve. Joy and gratitude ride hand in hand.

Friday is Friendship Friday. I have every single student get out of their desk and find someone they don't usually speak with. They are then supposed to tell this person one thing they like about themselves and something they like about the person they are speaking to. This positive affirmation session lasts a few minutes at the beginning of class. It's another day you can feel the joy of being kind to yourself and someone else. The kids really do enjoy Friendship Friday.

Similar to sending a message on social media asking for memorable moments from previous students and colleagues, I used a Google form and placed it on our learning management system for my current students. Some of the kids told me about Friendship Friday and how they have made new friends they probably wouldn't have ever spoken with if it weren't for this exercise.

During each class, I participate with the students. They see the joy in my eyes. I tell them what I am feeling and grateful for, and I participate in Friendship Friday. I'll randomly choose a kid and share with them. "Hey Bob, I like your shirt." "Hey, Jerry, I am digging those shoes." "Hey, Dylan, I am grateful to have you in my class today." Since I also participate, the kids see me as one of their own but as a teacher, too.

It only requires a few minutes a day.

If the joy and gratitude that are shared are falsified, they know it. I don't try to "fake it until I make it." I'm honest. When I am having a hard or a bad day, I explain. "Hey guys, I am having a hard day today, but I promise I will do my best to be the best kind teacher you deserve." I am genuinely open, and I am honest. They seem to appreciate my honesty, and I appreciate their appreciation.

So, what role does mindfulness play in the classroom, and why is it important to display and teach it? It is a journey within, and it is also a journey outside of yourself. It is a journey to meet people where they are. Everyone is in a different spot in their life. Everybody has a different thought process when it comes to mindfulness. That is okay. It really is. Variety is the spice of life.

A mindful administration is equally important to the faculty and staff. For instance, action-oriented meetings with open discussion and timeliness indicate that the administration understands its employees' needs. Is it a meeting that needs to occur to "check a box," or can it be handled via email? Is the meeting fun with interaction among the people in attendance? Is it a worthwhile meeting?

In addition, respectful administration works with their faculty and staff to plan for changes in curriculum and administrative processes. One of the most mindful schools I've taught at had small, incremental changes due to new teacher assessment guidelines. If they had us changed abruptly, it would have affected morale due to the sheer amount of work that had to be done to justify our positions. These slow changes allowed us to modify our activities deliberately and concisely instead of quickly without proper thought and planning. The changes were slowly phased in, and we were all much happier with the overall outcome. In opposition, one of the other schools in that district chose to abruptly change their assessment guidelines. There is no irony that they had a higher-than-usual staff turnover that year.

A mindful administration makes for happy, adjusted, and mindful faculty and staff: something that benefits the students, the school culture, the school district, and the community. Mindfulness is not something that is easily achievable, but it is worth every moment of vigorous attention.

I've added a new item to my teaching toolbox: my mindfulness journey. It appears to be benefiting both my students and me. As students have adjusted to my trustworthiness, genuineness, and humorousness, they have created their own "ness"—mindfulness.

I recognize that the students need a few minutes to react their minds after fighting overfilled hallways, bullying peers, and negative interactions. My classroom is a safe place, and these few minutes at the start of class demonstrate the respect that my children deserve. It's safe to unwind, be who you are, laugh, and make mistakes.

"Life is a dance. Mindfulness is witnessing that dance."

~ Amit Ray

Feelin' Whatcher Wednesday

When you change the way you look at things, the things you look at change.
Dr. Dyer

Beauty is being comfortable and confident in your own skin.

Chapter 8

Safety and Refuge

There seems to be a common theme in the vast number of comments students have made on social media about my classroom and teaching style: safety. They felt safe. I provided a safe environment for them to grow. I have always considered my classroom a safe space. Not in the protected from danger or violence type of security, but an emotional, psychological feeling of safety.

What makes you feel safe? What types of educators have made you feel safe? Did they appreciate you for who you are and let you revel in that knowledge? Did they give you a knowing glance to let you know they have faith in you?

What's the definition of safe? Safe is to be free from harm or secure from the threat of danger; it is also a place to protect valuables. Is the classroom a place to keep items of value? Aren't students valuable? Aren't their thoughts, feelings, and future invaluable and prized?

"Yes" is the answer to all these questions.

In addition, feeling safe may have different meanings for different people. Safety may mean clean water for washing hands, warm coffee, books to read, friends to share time with, a good meal, a warm blanket, and the smell of baking cookies. It is a feeling of being included and knowing that someone cares. According to the Psychology Today website, safety is a basic human need necessary for thriving relationships: a feeling of being accepted for who you are. There are physiological signs of feeling safe, such as a decreased heart rate, decreased respiratory rate, relaxed muscles, and even the ability to tolerate physical pain, which increases when someone feels safe.

Since I've defined the word "safe," let's look at some synonyms: intact, protected, secure, snug, cherished, guarded, unhurt, maintained, shielded, sheltered, under lock and key, under one's wing. I like snug, cherished, and under one's wing. These words make me feel cozy inside.

Throughout the years, I have taken students who were not in my class under my wing and helped nourish their spirits. Taylor was one of these students. Taylor, a high school senior who was fearless and inquisitive, used to sneak into my classroom from a neighboring room nearly every day. She loved to be in my room.

Her homeroom teacher was my neighboring colleague, and our classrooms had a doorway as a passage between them. He and I agreed that she could visit my room if Taylor finished her work in his class. Taylor was a brown-headed, brown-eyed senior who would light up a room each time she smiled. After Taylor had completed her classwork, she would cautiously tiptoe through the door and sit in one of the classroom or lab seats. Periodically, she would slip in during other class periods, and I would send her back to her class if it seemed inappropriate at the time.

Here is a quote from her Facebook post: "I remember that you were always a safe classroom to go to, always a safe and welcoming person. That truly mattered to me. I also remember how you'd invite everyone to come and learn about earth science, whether they were in your class or club or not. I would come over from Mr. Smith's class when I'd finished my work and learn from you. You taught me what eutrophication was in one of these classroom excursions." Those excursions were nearly daily, and I just loved having her learn with her peers. She especially enjoyed our labs and tended to help the lab groups if she had time. Taylor just never knew what we would do in class and hated missing out on the activities in my room. She now has her master's in marine biology, and I follow her blog posts and podcasts.

Another student mentioned that my room was a "safe space to express creativity," while others would wait on a brother or sister in my room after school. Some felt safe to rest, and many students felt it was a welcoming place to expand their passions and interests. During one school year, I agreed to sponsor the Auto Club. A group of students needed a safe space to discuss cars and plan a car show, and I was happy to provide that space.

No, I didn't, and I still don't know much about cars.

Just what was having a safe classroom? In my eyes, it was an environment where a student could use secret hand signals to indicate the need for extra help or to take a break due to anxiety. It involved a teacher recognizing a stressed student who needed to get up and move around. It was an environment where positive feedback was gloriously handed out. It was a setting where pupils could rest and be themselves. It was a place where they could cry when they needed a safe space to express themselves.

A safe classroom is an environment with a kind, empathetic, and loving teacher who exudes warmth while uplifting student expectations. It is somewhere that advocates faith in the future. It's where a frustrated person learns to accept assistance, particularly when they're out of steam. The safe classroom is an environment where there is joyful knowledge that our future will aspire toward its own greatness. It allows autonomy in projects and learning so students can discover on their own what they need to know—with a guide, not a dictatorial teacher. The safe classroom incorporates daily routine and provides a teacher with a compassionate presence and emotional steadiness. It encourages fun, joy, and humor.

The way I cultivated my classroom culture was like Doug Lemov's *Teach Like a Champion 3.0*. In addition, for many years, I have been using a variation of Dan Rothstein's and Luz Santana's Question Formulation Technique, as discussed in *Make Just One Change*. The Question Formulation Technique (QFT) was created by the Right Question Institute (rightquestion.org). As I began to write this book, I reviewed these two guidebooks to teaching, and I realized I had already created a "culture of error" in my classroom while I taught my students the question formulation technique. A "culture of error" is a technique to check students' understanding of concepts covered in class. Many teachers, if not most teachers, objectively base assessments of understanding with questions and answer sessions where there are right or wrong answers. They also tend to assess understanding with quizzes and tests.

Creating a culture of error actively observes student progress by observing misconceptions and correcting incorrect facts with student-led question creation and discussion.

By expecting students to respect each other and modeling that respect, students became willing to "step outside of the box" and offer, then discuss questions being posed during class. I was notorious for offering a plethora of choices and allowing the students to formulate new questions. Students then discussed the validity of each choice when a question had been asked. This tended to lead to a detailed problem-solving activity where they were required to figure out why each choice was correct, incorrect, or required more research. I always followed up with positive praise for the risk-takers and would eventually reveal the proper answer. These types of question-and-answer sessions taught me as much as the students. I discovered their thought processes on the subject and could correct them as needed.

Students became well-versed in this technique within a few weeks of the start of school. Students became comfortable and began asking relevant questions. Oh, how I loved to answer the questions with their own questions to make them think critically about topics!

Why did I use this technique? They learned to not be fearful of failing. My classroom instilled a learning culture of trying and adjusting the technique needed for long-term memory, not just memorization. They learned how to use that knowledge in some way, shape, or form.

In my classroom, students were openly grateful, knowing that someone had a fishing lure in their pond, a stake in their success. It was something I enjoyed immensely. By normalizing mistakes and creating a safe environment, I helped them grow by nurturing their inner curiosity. The innate wish to learn and do more is natural, a process of growth and change. I ensured that each student knew I believed in their abilities and would give them a safe place to be brave and experiment with those essential qualities of spirit and mind. As a result, students who had moved on from my classes would come to my room for a daily hug, fist bump, or lunch.

My favorite hugs were from another big, burly football player named Jaden. He came by every day for a quick hug and always said, "I love you, Doc," as he left my room. Yes, I know he felt safe in my presence and in my classroom.

What else made my kids feel safe? I encouraged them to let me know when I had erred. After all, I'm not faultless. These errors could be simple typos, grade omissions, or strange test questions—any mistake I took to heart, and I truly investigated it. I appreciated having hundreds watching out for slipped keyboard mistakes, grading bumbles, and mathematical mistakes. The only request I made of the students was that they point out errors in a respectful manner and submit them to me in written form. Students generally followed through with a quickly typed email or lengthy explanation of why a question on a quiz or test was inaccurate.

Feeling safe doesn't apply only to the classroom. What about school functions or club activities? My students knew I was dependable and felt safe under my wing, whether it be competition trips within the city or statewide.

I have fond memories of driving to multiple destinations with one of the officers for Health Occupation Students of America (HOSA), a student-led club I sponsored. Her name was Amelia, and we traveled back and forth across the state to different conferences and competitive sites. We became very close during that time and learned to trust and feel safe in each other's presence.

After a four-day trip to the state conference, we were both utterly exhausted. I had a six-hour drive ahead of us, and we stopped to load up on caffeine multiple times. We chatted, sang songs, discussed classes, and reveled in her time in HOSA. Amelia's emotions were bittersweet because she loved being the president that year, although she was also relieved that the responsibilities had been passed on to another student. About halfway through the last trip together, as I was driving late that night, I began talking about how grateful I was for our time together. When she didn't respond, I realized she was snoring softly. I giggled to myself and let her sleep. In my mind, I'm sure she heard my words that night.

Throughout the years, students felt safe digging in the dirt on a Sunday afternoon or washing cars at a fundraiser on a Saturday morning. Students were comfortable asking me uncomfortable questions and sending emails late at night. They knew they would not be ridiculed, harassed, or made to feel silly. Most of the time, I would respond via email when I got to school in the morning, but sometimes, they would receive a response at 4:30 in the morning, followed up with a silly emoji.

In contrast, if someone feels unsafe, they lack emotional safety. The real you feels unloved after being belittled, ignored, or emotionally attacked. When this occurs, your brain doesn't know the difference between physical and emotional danger and responds in kind.

What do you feel when you are emotionally threatened? Do your muscles tense? Do you feel as if you want to lash out? Do you feel pain in some way? Your brain does all of that and more when it is under attack on an emotional level.

How does safety, both physically and psychologically, apply to an employee within a school? What role do supervisors and administration play?

At one school, a supervisor tended to micromanage her faculty. She seemed to enjoy unexpectedly entering the classroom to observe and rate teacher performance based on how well the lesson plan was followed. At this time, my lesson plans were not as streamlined as described in the chapter about trust. During one of these unannounced observations, she noticed I had changed my lessons that day. Based on student need, I decided to reteach a specific concept in chemistry due to the student's confusion. During this class, she raised her hand and asked why I was not following my original lesson plans, basically interrupting class.

As a result of her observation, I was required to write a formal report explaining my reasons for the modification, which was due the next day, or it would have affected my exemplary rating. I missed an activity with my daughter and could not help my eldest child with his homework that night due to the requirements of this report. At the time, it felt as if I had been attacked, and I did not feel safe on either a personal or professional level.

In contrast, another administrator at another school knew that lesson plans were plans and changes needed to occur based on the students' needs. She saw it as a good trait to be able to redesign lessons as required. This made me feel safe due to being trusted as a professional..

Let's talk about the time that we had a gun safety threat at a campus where I taught. We were expected to maintain a calm atmosphere with our students as we awaited instructions. Imagine my surprise when one of the administrators started screeching angrily at a group of teachers I was standing with: "I said move to the back of the building." She was red-faced, flailing her arms and running around the school parking lot. We were all quite flustered and scared due to this safety threat and it was unnecessary to yell at us. This episode was a clear example of an upset administrator who did not have the tools to keep her students and staff feeling safe.

I take pride in making others feel safe, valuable, and exceptional. I find joy in the knowledge that students throughout the years have recognized that I worked hard to be considered trustworthy, genuine, humorous, and mindful while providing a safe space for all to enjoy. But how do they learn in my room?

I am a science teacher, and we wear lab coats, immerse ourselves in hands-on learning, and problem-solving, and do oodles and oodles of labs!

"Education breeds confidence. Confidence breeds hope. Hope breeds peace."

~ Confucius

Chapter 9

Lab Coats, Paint, and Creative Problem Solving

Marie Montessori stated, "Do not tell them how to do it. Show them how to do it, and do not say a word. If you tell them, they will watch your lips move. If you show them, they will want to do it themselves."

Students learn to think critically by using the scientific method in my class. After all, I do teach science. The scientific method is a way to solve problems that involve steps that start by identifying a problem and asking questions. Then, research occurs. Students research the problem they have identified, determine the components involved, and identify something that can be modified and tested to see if it solves the problem. A hypothesis has been formed at this point. Students then decide the best way to test that hypothesis and then do the testing. Results must be shared with peers and me as the teacher.

Problem-solving can be messy since it is a process of trial and error. Once the kids have developed the skills to follow through with this process, they love it.

Let's return to a variation of the question from earlier. What did your teacher do that helped you feel empowered to learn? Did they give you autonomy over your learning? Did they allow you to make decisions as you traversed new material?

Alexandra, an artist, and curious person, had read that water bears can live in very harsh environments and asked me if she could experiment with locating them from the oak trees outside my classroom. Through problem-solving and multiple attempts using different supplies, she found Tardigrades, also known as water bears, as she used a microscope. She told me years later that it was a "magical experience, and they were so cute." I had allowed Alexandra the freedom to experiment on a subject she was interested in and ask her own questions as she followed through to fruition. This allowed her to learn on her own with general guidance from me. Her lab report was an amazing piece of artwork that demonstrated what she did and what she saw. She now works at a zoo, doing what she loves. I'm not surprised due to her huge heart and love of animals.

Another student, Micky, loved making videos and created a fanciful one demonstrating environmental issues with hypothesized solutions. As part of this video, I pushed her to be authentic and demonstrate her sense of humor to make it more interesting. Her sense of humor was like mine: questionable and outrageous. She recently revealed, "You let us use a soundtrack of Owen Wilson saying 'wow' over and over again over a serious environmental video. I was genuinely touched by how much freedom and fun you let your students have. You were the coolest teacher!"

Cool, um. Maybe.

These are two examples of how I allowed students to make choices in their learning using the skills they learned from me as the teacher. These students had legitimate learning experiences and gained a full understanding of the curriculum as they studied something of interest to them.

When you were in school, did you do science labs, have field trips, write poetry, expand upon knowledge with videos, create art, and problem-solve individually or with groups? In my class, you do all those things and a great deal more, like making fudge using weird chemistry formulas and cooking eggs without heat. One of my former students sent me a video she posted on Facebook of my shenanigans trying to get those darned eggs to cook. My chemistry demonstrations were performed similarly to my cooking style, needing "a little more of this and a little more of that."

Please don't judge. This was the first year I taught chemistry, and we were all having fun as I relearned the material.

Lab days were fun days. I opened this book with a statement made more times than I care to remember. "Don't lick that" has been said as much as "Don't put that in your mouth." I wonder if the essence of students' pasts echoes through my classroom, and it causes the boys, sometimes girls, to want to eat something gross—for five dollars—during labs.

Labs took a bit of work. I had to remind students of proper behavior and expectations, and of course, it required plenty of preparatory work on my end. Every moment of prep work was worth the effort since the kids were up, moving around, taking care of their group responsibilities, asking questions, and doing their assignments. They were trusted to learn. All while having fun!

Over the past few years, the courses have been dissection intensive, so labs have included eyeballs, kidneys, brains, hearts, and larger specimens. Don't worry. I won't go into detail due to squeamish stomachs. I'll allow your imagination to take care of this part of what I currently do for a living.

A few of the multitude of hands-on activities included mimicking the digestive system with pantyhose, bread, vinegar, and baking soda. Their faces were hilarious as they performed peristalsis with their hands. Mushing the ball of food down the hosiery to the end generally caused at least one boy to make gagging noises. When the bolus of food would reach the end of the hose, someone had the honor of pushing it out of a cut hole. Oh yeah, kids tried to eat that too.

Have you ever heard of the acronym STEAM? It stands for Science, Technology, Engineering, Art, and Mathematics. I'm all for acronyms, but come on, that seems excessive. Art expression is used in many cultures to help express and deliver a product or service. Just look at the cover of this book. Is there art in a museum? What about anatomy and physiology coloring books? I can guarantee that every medical professional you have ever seen has colored human body parts in an anatomy coloring book at some point.

When you give students large sheets of butcher paper and a list of bones they must draw into a life-size outline of a group member, they are usually bewildered. After a while, they figure out what to do, and I let them run with it. When the group member that has been outlined gets up, there's usually plenty of giggling because of the absurdity of the drawings. One girl outlined a boy's pants and large shirt and decided to make the skeleton into Frankenstein. I think it turned out spectacular!

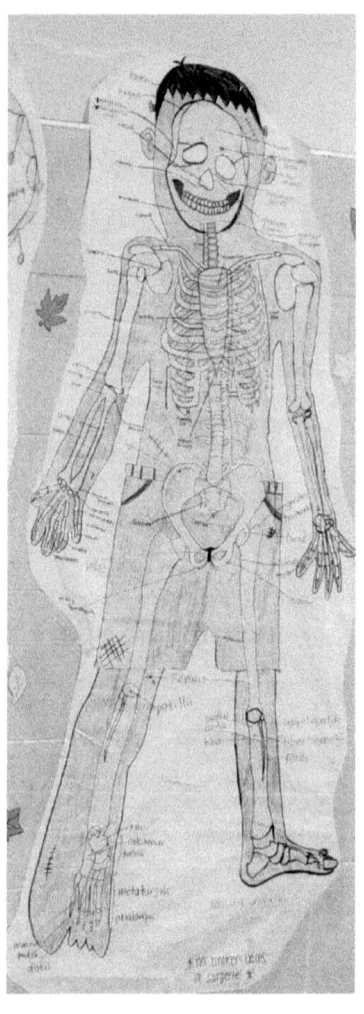

They were learning the bones and how the bones fit together on their own through art. Another Marie Montessori quote that displays the importance of students self-teaching is, "The greatest sign of success for a teacher is to be able to say, "The children are now working as if I did not exist.'" I guided them, acting as counsel only by pointing out obvious errors and reminding them of expectations. Once the students completed their skeletal works of art, I displayed them in the hallway as Halloween decorations and then placed a construction paper Santa hat on each skull for the Christmas holidays.

Students have had a wide variety of art activities, from water painting nervous system cells to 3-D models, commercials, posters of all kinds, and videos. Experiences that intertwine science and art are memorable, especially when I post them outside the classroom for all to appreciate. How do I benefit on a personal level? I get to see who my true artists are.

I love these activities.

Problem-solving with a little guidance is also a great activity, although it isn't something that I have success with at the beginning of each year. The students must be taught to create solutions to problems as they create and answer relevant questions. They need to learn to work hard, trust themselves, and develop their work ethic, knowing I will guide them.

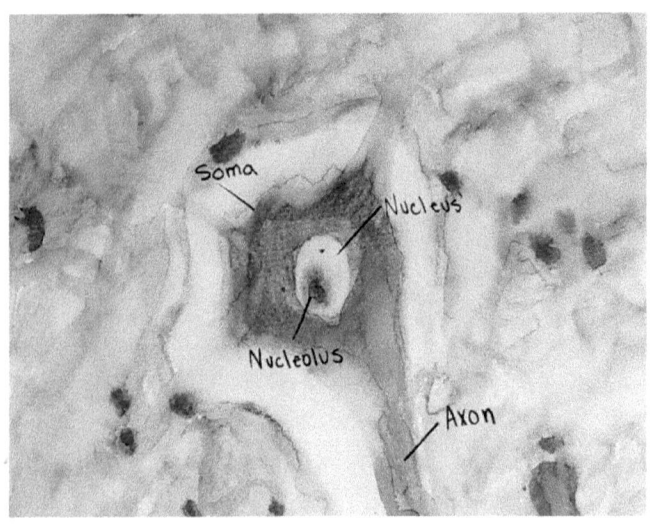

I regularly used case studies in biological classes as problem-solving activities. Students were assigned a case study based on the organ system we were covering. The case studies included diagnostic tests, signs, and symptoms of an ill patient. Students, usually in groups, were assigned to determine what was wrong with the patient based on references and class discussion. Boy, did they argue over potential diseases!

It was like music to my ears. They fully engaged in the activity by researching, discussing the patient's issues, and creating solutions. Once again, they were actively learning on their own.

In pathophysiology, I asked how the students wanted to be tested over the unit we were about to wrap up. Since assessments don't always have to be tests, I wanted their opinion because I valued their input. Groups or singletons were then assigned to figure out the normal anatomy and design a disease that wasn't in their book or easily found online. Signs, symptoms, tests, treatments, and patient outcomes were all demonstrated as part of their student-centered learning.

What did this have to do with being trustworthy, genuine, humorous, and mindful while providing a safe environment?

Everything!

I trusted them to complete the assignment. They felt safe asking questions, and they felt that I had a genuine interest in their learning. They knew I would be aware of and recognize signs of disinterest or frustration, and I would guide them to look beyond such feelings, usually with good-natured humor. They knew I would consult with them but not do their work. They also knew of the high expectations and that I intended for them to meet those expectations. This included using relevant references if they chose to use sites other than the ones I had provided. You could usually hear me spit out, "Don't go to Aliens.com to look for answers. It isn't a relevant website." Students usually responded with an eye roll or giggle.

During all projects, I accepted that students may choose to learn alone or in small groups. I am a private learner and prefer to learn independently, so I understood how the singletons felt.

I gave them the freedom to choose how to present the information they had learned, and I worked with them to create grading rubrics for their projects. How could they present? Videos, posters, websites, 3D objects, booklets, pamphlets, songs, videos, and poems are examples of how students could present the data they had learned. I allowed them autonomy and trusted them to have a stake in their learning and future.

How did I lead them to apply higher-level learning? Each unit started as many teachers begin, with fifteen to twenty minutes of instructive lectures and assignments that complemented the lecture. Quizzes and sometimes tests were given, and then they were taught how to complete the upcoming project. They needed guidance to fulfill the expectations of the forthcoming activity. They couldn't read my mind!

I must admit that a lot of educators find this challenging. Giving up open control of a classroom full of teenagers was difficult, but it was effective and continues to be effective. At first, I found this challenging, but I was helped along the way by a remarkable administrator from a prior school district, for which I will always be thankful.

True student-centeredness is the allowance of student-created questions and experimentation with their own learning. This is achievable if students receive instruction and know they can ask questions in a safe setting without fear of rejection or scorn. For there to be trust between students and teachers in the classroom, there needs to be mutual respect between them.

The "Infamous Flat Lorax" is what one student called a project we did in Environmental Science. I was one of the first teachers who became involved with a project that became the National Flat Lorax Project. It was an environmental science project that took ideas from both *The Lorax* by Dr. Seuss and the Flat Stanley Project to create a collaborative and unique task for students. They had to observe their surroundings and write about what they saw, both positive and negative.

Do you remember the Lorax? He's a hairy, short orange fellow who "speaks for the trees." A remake of the original 1970s cartoon video was recreated in 2012. Personally, I don't have the same affinity for the remake as for the shorter version from my childhood.

Pupils were directed to create and color a Flat Lorax, take a picture with the Flat Lorax somewhere environmentally relevant, and write a letter about their trip and the importance of the site. Some students went to the zoo, others wrote about trash on the side of the road, and one even took his Flat Lorax dove hunting. Many wrote about the lack of recycling on campus.

I did not require them to make a special trip somewhere, but many chose to use it as an adventure with their friends. Some of their pictures were quite entertaining.

Students were required to mail these to respective schools that fellow teachers across the country organized. Each student shared their experiences on the due date and was handed envelopes to address. Imagine a group of about twenty-five seventeen and eighteen-year-olds holding the envelopes with looks of confusion on their faces.

I came to a realization. They didn't know how to address envelopes. What I would call an essential life skill was lacking. Who would have thought that addressing envelopes would be part of a twelfth-grade class? This turned out to be much more of an issue than I had expected. When you *textify* an address, it won't reach the destination. Leaving off a city, transposing zip code numbers, and not realizing the importance of a street address was mystifying to them.

Teachers are assessed annually, which requires an administrator to fill out paperwork and observe them in their classroom. Usually, the observation date is scheduled well in advance to avoid test days. When I am observed, I typically ask the administrator to ask the students what we are doing; they nearly always know, which is a sign of a teacher with high marks.

Many of my peers put on a "dog and pony" show for administrators, not demonstrating what truly happens in the classroom daily. My viewpoint on this matter may differ since I entered teaching within an alternative certification program and had weekly observations.

There wasn't time to schedule dog and pony shows or create show-stopping lessons. I just taught and let my colleagues with experience guide me.

This chapter hasn't included positives or negatives about administration for a reason. These are my activities and my pupils, and very few activities in my classroom have ever been affected by good or bad administration.

So, how do peers and colleagues play a role in my classroom? I have good stories and, well, not-so-pleasant stories to share.

"If we are truly effective teachers, then we are creating autonomous, independent, and self-directed learners."

~ Robert John Meehan

Chapter 10

Collaboration with Counterparts

I frantically ran into Sebastian's classroom. "Dude, I need some microscope slides." Sebastian pointed to the lab area and said, "Help yourself."

"Where are they?" I asked.

He replied while pointing to the left, "Over there."

Yeah, that was not very helpful, but not unexpected. His lab appeared neat and clean, but you risked your life when a drawer or cabinet was opened. I loved working with Sebastian. As another outspoken "quirky" science teacher, he and I got along fabulously most of the time.

We shared a storage closet and door between our classrooms. I always had bits and pieces of projects stored on my side of the storage closet that looked like the drawers in his classroom—stuff was everywhere. One day, I went in, and he was clearing my materials out of the storeroom. I was livid and started hauling materials back into the storeroom while firmly and repeatedly stating, "Not waste—it can be reused!" I tended to hoard potential project materials like screws, wood, paint, cardboard, and packing material. After my temper tantrum ended and due to his calming influence, I realized that I needed to declutter the mess because we were both tripping over a bunch of useless crap when we entered the storage area.

Sebastian was always a surprise. One day, he decided to clean our lab freezer and use an ice pick instead of defrosting it. That went as well as it sounds. I heard him repeatedly jabbing at something, saying "S..." and then a whoosh sound. The ice pick was dangling from the wall of the freezer. Replacing that appliance was a chunk out of the budget that year.

Peers and colleagues can be frustrating but innovative and inspiring at the same time. Olivia, my first mentor, was instrumental in my growth as an educator during my first year as a teacher. She guided me out of the "sit and get" sessions my students were forced to endure. You must know that I had only been a college student and had an office as a chiropractor after graduation from college. I didn't have the average new teacher experience since I went through an alternative certification program to achieve my teaching credentials. I was thrust into the classroom with rudimentary training as a teacher.

My poor students at the time sat and took notes from an overhead projector with labs splashed in here and there. Olivia was instrumental in integrating labs and lectures and helped me learn how to work with a team. She also showed me how to set personal boundaries with students.

Boundaries? A handful of students liked to stay late, usually until five o'clock, for tutorials every day after school. My official tutorial days and times were Monday, Wednesday, and Thursday until four o'clock. I felt that this group of students required guidance and extra help. I also enjoyed having them work and ask questions after school. I felt like they needed me. The problem was that to prepare for the next school day properly, I had to stay after they left. This would make for an extraordinarily long school day since I arrived at about 6:30 a.m. each day.

At one of our mentor/mentee meetings, Olivia mentioned setting strict guidelines regarding tutorial times, or I may become burned out early in the school year. I vehemently denied that I would grow weary of my newly founded career but took it to heart later in the conversation when she mentioned that it appeared that I may have enabled the students.

Enabled? I learned from her that a small group of students began to feel they were unable to complete their homework assignments without my assistance. They were ninth-grade students who still didn't know how to schedule themselves or how to learn on their own.

At the time, I didn't realize that this one conversation would mold my educational philosophy, which includes guiding students to embrace education in the form that best suits them. I facilitate as they learn how to make connections when they learn content and concepts by discovering their own why and how through problem-solving and critical thinking. Yes, I know, this is student-centered learning. I was learning how to guide and facilitate long before school districts thought it was cool.

It was difficult for me to say "No" that first year, but I learned how to set boundaries and begin to actually teach the students, not dictate in their general direction. I will always be grateful for Olivia's guidance.

Later, I became an active participant in groups of teams that collaborated to design lessons that were active and fun for everyone in the classroom. We were like professional cohorts that worked together like a well-oiled machine. We split the workload, shared ideas, and worked towards helping the students who struggled the most. Some days, the meetings seemed to drag on for hours, and at the time, I didn't appreciate the time spent, but now I know there is great value in integrated collaboration.

After being a member of a truly inspiring and fully functional team, it is difficult to accept anything less. This experience was key to becoming a team leader, department chair, and district team leader later in my career.

How do collaborative teams benefit students? Teams help to form a bridge between the curriculum and us as teachers. This, in turn, leads the students to valuable learning experiences. When teachers form a good working relationship, students know what is expected from a class. For example, there were nine biology teachers at one campus. Biology was a ninth-grade class, so the students were new to high school. Based on our conversations and classroom observations, we discovered that students were struggling due to misunderstanding how to develop their own study skills. As a team, we decided to instill study skills as part of our curriculum. Before covering biology content each day, we implemented mini-lessons until we felt the students had become active participants in the development of their study skills.

This benefited the students in all classes, not just biology.

We had created a battle plan that would minimally interrupt our curricular requirements, and we installed that plan. In addition, our biology team created a systematic grading system and a plan for similar lessons, organized our distribution of lab supplies, and created common assessments such as quizzes and tests.

We each had our own backgrounds, interests, and talents to which we actively contributed. We shamelessly shared materials with each other and respected that we all had our own teaching style.

This was a smooth-running, efficient group of mature adults who openly worked together so our students could reach their full potential. This is a team I yearned for when I no longer taught biology. Our collaboration benefited all of our students.

Isn't that the purpose of a team in an educational environment?

I have always gotten along with my colleagues, with a rare disagreement throughout the years. Unfortunately, there was a time when I had negative experiences with colleagues who were unwilling to work as a team and who were generally unfriendly when asked to share. I will never understand why that group of teachers felt it was okay to not be inclusive in unity as a team. We all did our own thing, which regularly caused confusion among students, especially students who had to exchange teachers due to schedule changes.

Administration plays an essential role in modeling and implementing expectations for teams. If those guidelines are unreasonable and unrealistic, this affects morale and overall lesson planning. For instance, I was required to host team meetings with my science teachers for an hour each week at one campus, but none of us taught the same course. We had overarching goals for our students; outside of that, the meetings were futile and a waste of time. We couldn't formulate lesson plans or spend time productively. Meetings with this team were important, but not for an hour weekly. This particular year, a micro-managing administrator was attending our meetings. It's a good thing I took acting lessons as a child. I believe that is what got us through that mess since there was definitely a lot of blah, blah, blah.

My background includes specialized subjects. During most of my career, I've been a singleton, the only person who taught a subject at the school, sometimes within the whole district. Being a singleton without a team to brainstorm with and discuss daily mundane topics can be lonely and distressing. Although I was surrounded by hundreds of students per day, they were not educated colleagues. Partners of equal status were needed to help each day run smoothly.

Having equals and peers to chat with and share responsibilities with is vital during the school day. Teaching is very stressful, and camaraderie can help alleviate the mental stresses felt. Whether it be a jokester teacher who randomly turned off my classroom overhead light during the middle of the school day, shared frustration when a printer went offline, or delivered copies to a fellow teacher, companionship eased mental anxiety, achieved a feeling of connectedness and decreased feelings of depression and despondency. We all need cohorts to share our various stories, whether those stories are positive, negative, or somewhere in between.

I'm not a readily social person by nature. I have a tiny bubble of trusted family and friends, but I still need accepting, friendly, cordial coworkers to share a smile, a joke, or at least someone to share a knowing glance with during a challenging day. I've been fortunate to have that throughout my career, with the exception I shall explain below.

I suppose it is partly my fault. I tried to form a cohesive, specialized, collaborative team where we could work together to better our respective programs. Unfortunately, the "team" I attempted to build didn't agree and ousted me as the administratively appointed leader. Their excuse? We didn't teach the same classes, so we weren't a team, and therefore, we didn't need a team leader.

I respectfully disagree.

I was flabbergasted at the response and am still unsure why they were adamantly against working with me. Perhaps it was due to contrary experiences while on a team in the past. Maybe they thought I was trying to control them? Perhaps they didn't like me because I didn't spend time passing rumors with them during lunch?

Regardless of my colleague's reasoning, administration should have had my back and installed some form of team within our educational program. It wasn't necessary for me to be the team leader, but someone should have done something to right this wrong. Our supervisor should have proactively taken the helm to steer the boat so we could be laser-focused on student success as a team.

Even a mediocre administrator could have stepped in to avoid the floundering resulting from my rejection as the team leader. That mediocrity hadn't been met, and I became the hapless recipient of the most adversarial workplace I had ever experienced.

At the beginning of this ill-disposed school year, I was not expecting to confront a transition away from a high school teaching career, not yet. Now, I'm open to leaving, and I have no craving to reapply at another school district and start over. Teaching in public schools has left a nasty taste in my mouth, a foul foreboding of dread due to the knowledge that this lack of support is widespread. It was never this bad in the past, at least in my experience. I've merely been fortunate to be hired by innovative schools. Once again, I am grateful for those experiences. I have tried to explain to new teachers that many schools were not this negligent in their support. These green newbies didn't believe me and consistently left quietly without explanation at the end of the school year. This has led to a shortage of qualified, passionate, and empowered educators at this particular school.

The purpose of having a team is to create a culture of collaboration. When teams don't join together due to misunderstandings, personality conflicts, or more serious issues such as bias, it affects the atmosphere inside and outside the classroom.

During my roughest years as a teacher, drama unfolded. Behavior I didn't understand toward myself, fellow teachers, and students occurred. Combativity, screaming, and open hostility focused on me and my students became daily occurrences. I began to struggle with my mental health and desperately tried to focus on each moment to make it through the day—days I used to enjoy immensely.

As the quandary unfolded on my campus, I asked for administrative assistance to help navigate the emotional turmoil brewing. In addition, I spent a great deal of time reading about how to heal wounds and recreate communication channels after those channels had been damaged. As a result, I tried to mend fences to no avail. It was a challenge to focus on mindfulness due to the negativity I experienced each day, and I reverted to self reflection—a reflection of my actions and how I could better the situation.

Only after students and parents filed official complaints did the administration finally step in to rectify the situation. Halfway through the school year, an administrative team attempted to enforce a team atmosphere. If an outsider had looked in, it would have appeared to have fixed the problem of unprofessionalism and the contentious attitudes of my colleagues. As an insider, I can verify that it was a superficial fix at best.

In contrast, I've had warm peers, colleagues, and teams, whether in person, via Zoom, email, or online collaboration. Remember the Flat Lorax? Sebastian? Olivia? How about the multitudes of exceptional individuals I've been blessed to work with in the past? I've had trust and genuinely complimentary interactions with colleagues and peers, even with an administration that isn't healthy.

Teaching is always stressful, and it is helpful to have favorable morale shared with colleagues: people to laugh with when opening supplies for a newly built lab, someone to vent to when frustrated, or someone to bounce ideas off of. All are invaluable when embroiled in a stressful career.

During the COVID-19 experience, especially at the start, there was a plethora of collaboration between teachers and administration. How the hell would we flip to online learning when most of us had little to no experience with this type of technology? We worked day and night together to make it work, and I feel my kids didn't miss much of the curriculum. Maybe they lost the ability to manage their time and keep up with the assignments, but not a loss of learning. I still use some of the techniques I learned to teach online in the classroom today.

On a side note, the kids' technological savvy has created fresh, inventive ways for them to cheat. I'm so glad we have paper! Compared to digital learning, I've seen that information retention increases when assignments are turned in on paper, and the pupils themselves confess that they prefer to switch back to paper.

In summary, peer and colleague interaction can help or hamper your ability as an educator. From assisting with lab materials to guiding as a mentor, relationships with colleagues can make or break a person's ability to be less pressured and better at their job—to teach and guide students to find their interests and excel within their talent stream. Basically, an empathetic and compassionate administration should exemplify support from the top down. Without this support, teachers move on, leave, change schools, and eventually leave the profession.

"No task is too great, no accomplishment too grand, no dream too far-fetched for a team. It takes teamwork to make the dream work."

~ John Maxwell

Chapter 11

School Administrative Stewardship

I f you are an educator, you will understand much of what has been written in this book. But, if not, let me express my gratitude for you making it this far. I can only assume that you have read this book out of curiosity, concern for a family member or friend, or perhaps to understand the public education dilemma you read and hear about in the news and on social media.

It is said that "When a principal sneezes, the entire school gets a cold." I find this quite accurate. How so?

If the highest administration on campus is compassionate and understanding and works to ensure a positive morale and work environment, the school can recuperate from negativity quickly. The same is true for an administration that is mediocre or lacking in ability:

the school will not be resilient to setbacks and will allow uncertainty and cynicism to wreak havoc on its faculty, staff, and students.

Unhealthy administration micromanages and doesn't treat their faculty as professionals by reminding them of the contract hours each day. Unhealthy administration dismisses student concerns regarding problematic teachers. Unhealthy administration allows redundancy and doubling, even tripling of workloads by requiring multiple copies and uploads of paperwork, where one form could take care of the requirements. Unhealthy administration requires unmeaningful meetings when an email or memo could easily convey the message. Unhealthy administration loves reminding faculties that daily struggle is always "for the kids." An unhealthy administration causes a school to have sickly morale, hurting the students as they learn to navigate life.

Healthy administration allows the most feared assistant principal to be duct taped to the wall to raise money for a school garden. Healthy administration brings in a set of massage therapists for ten-minute massages during teacher appreciation week. Healthy administration allows school personnel assistance covering a class when they want to donate blood at a blood drive. Healthy administration allows teacher input and takes it seriously. Healthy administration allows growth and assistance to those struggling and needing extra support. Healthy administration respects an educator's time and doesn't allow meetings that could be handled with an email; if a meeting is required, it is meaningful. A healthy administration recovers quickly from adversity, which assists students to learn resiliency.

Does any of this make sense to you? A good administrative team is just as important as good leadership in business. I'll do my best to expand upon this point.

Let's say you have an angry, disruptive coworker. If this is reported and this behavior continues, in the typical business world, the employee may wind up being transferred, demoted, or fired at some point. The boss will probably take the complaints seriously and work to remove that person from the work environment due to disruption of morale, thus affecting productivity. The worthiness of an employee in a business setting is up to the employee to justify. If they want that job, the employee must change any angry, disruptive, or inappropriate behavior, at least during working hours.

The proof of wrongdoing in education is on the person making the complaint. A complainant must prove that they have done everything within their power to fix the situation before involving an overworked administrator. This means meetings, battle plans, plans of action, more meetings, more battle plans, and more action plans. I understand everyone is busy, but more meetings and discussions are not the answer when all prospects of resolving the conflict have advanced without resolution.

Administration must step in to amend the situation in haste with a guarantee of more than a slap on the wrist.

I've witnessed the above many times during my educational career, and I have supported colleagues who have been wrongly treated. Due to the sheer amount of work required when filing complaints and grievances against colleagues, I've done my best to avoid making official complaints.

In addition, the retribution factor is real. I have seen emotions taken out on colleagues and innocent students throughout my years in education. Students who have tried to make good choices by filing appropriate complaints were unfairly placed in detention and failed during the complaint process. A functional administration would have moved the students to another class instead of allowing them to be harassed in the classroom.

What was my solution for survival during the tumultuous school year referred to earlier in this book? t was simple: I was there for the kids, my students. I continued to be a role model, taught them to trust through my actions, showed them how important it is to be genuine, modeled stress relief healthily, and, most importantly, showed them unconditional love and support. I hope they learned they were worthy of that love without having to prove themselves. I did all of the above every day while teaching the curriculum and living in a hate-filled, toxic work environment. I wanted them to be successful in the future.

It wasn't simple. It was painful, and I endured it for the sake of my students.

You may wonder why I didn't go to my union for assistance in matters not conducive to learning and positivity in the school atmosphere. We don't have teacher unions in my state. We do not have that kind of representation. The kind of representation that we have involves membership in groups that lead at the state level, not at the individual level. Membership has perks, such as saving money on car insurance, receiving discounts on rental cars, and access to education attorneys. It was like a paid retainer or very expensive insurance. If you are wondering, I contacted an attorney as part of the complaint process and explicitly followed his advice.

As stated above, I have spent a lot of time reflecting and decided to research school philosophies around the world. I happened upon Neil and Jane Hawke's *The Inner Curriculum* and have become inspired to share the concepts that have been put into place in countries such as England, Australia, Sweden, India, and New Zealand. The curriculum teaches pupils *Values-based Education* in an effort to make students more interconnected with humanity and the natural world. To help them experience enhanced well-being by "developing traits that contribute to the wellbeing of others and our world." This, in turn, increases resilience by being "conscious and in harmonious control of their internal world of thoughts, feelings, and emotions."

The curriculum is based on psychotherapy practices and interpersonal neurobiology. It has been implemented in many schools, such as Fielding Primary School in London, Academia Britanica Cuscatleca in El Salvador, Snells Beach School in New Zealand, and Heneskolan, Skövde in Sweden. Valuesbasededucation.com has a wide selection of information to read and learn from, and I have explored their curriculum with voracity. I've even begun experimenting with using value-based verbiage as part of the mindfulness journey I've implemented at the beginning of each class. Terms such as imagination, trust, reflection, openness, and cooperation have been used as the students meditate, perform yoga, express feelings, write a mini journal of gratitude, and make new friends.

The teachings of *Values-based Education* focus on the child, the teacher, the staff, and the surroundings, such as the school building and parking lot. As part of implementing these teachings, faculty think more deeply about their teachings and are aware of the values that they model both in and out of the classroom. Mental health can be enhanced, and choice-making can be reflective, which leads to a feeling of connection to others and, thus, the world. Achievements by using *Values-based Education* can create a positive learning environment for all people within a school. This includes students, staff, faculty, and administrators. I've become enthralled with the possibilities this program could lead to when applied within a school environment. I would love to see this style of education implemented in the United States. Doesn't it sound extraordinary?

Back to how healthy schools react to those in need.

How can a healthy administration assist students who need help? Welcome to the story of Leo, a defiant but highly intelligent young man. He was the middle child of a suburban household, and didn't fit into the same mold as his older sister and younger brother. Leo's siblings were diligent and successful students with high grades, and both were very active in the band program and participated in multiple honor societies.

Leo was different. He didn't see himself in the same category as his siblings, and he was correct. He was a courageous youth who aspired to be a famous magician one day. Grades were not important to him. He was gifted with the ability to be charismatic and optimistic, and I always enjoyed his presence in my class, although his behavior could be problematic.

During his senior year of high school, I pulled him aside because of his failing grades. He usually kept his grades hovering around a C, but he had completely stopped doing his homework and seemed distracted during class.

During our conversation, I discovered that he heavily pushed his parents' buttons, and they sent him packing to find his own way. They had thrown him out of the house. He had concealed his plight with an ingenious survival plan, for he always arrived on time to school in clean clothes, freshly showered and fed. For the past three weeks, he had been sleeping on the roof of a neighboring school, using the gym showers, and stealing breakfast from the school's cafeteria. He would ride his bike to school, attend classes, and then go to work at a small restaurant down the road, where he would eat his dinner while at work. At closing time, he would ride his bike to a club or park, play his guitar, and demonstrate his magic card tricks for spare change. He would then return to that neighboring school, sleep on the roof, and repeat the cycle. I was aghast but somehow found a way to hide my feelings.

He was not perturbed whatsoever. It was a game to him, a game of survival, and he felt he was winning this dangerous game. He was having fun. Although his resilience was inspiring, I was terrified for his safety and well-being.

Based on his body posture, I was afraid he would run if he knew what I was about to do, so I sent him to his next class with explicit instructions to return to my class after school for a soda before going to work. I promptly asked a colleague to watch my class while I sprinted to the counseling office to explain the situation. Just as I felt, they were appalled by Leo's situation and began making phone calls to his parents and the authorities. I was not privy to these conversations, but I know what happened next on Leo's life journey.

As it turned out, Leo had a good relationship with his aunt, who helped him move into her home. She agreed that he could continue his employment at the restaurant but had to stop asking for change after it closed. She began picking him up at the restaurant after his shift because he tended not to follow her instructions.

At first, he was not pleased with my actions or the efforts of the school to help him. I assume he thought his aunt would eventually throw him out of the house, but she didn't, and he graduated a few months later. I lost track of Leo and wondered what happened to him and his rambunctious spirit.

This is how a healthy administration behaves when a student is in need. They led him to safety with their hearts. The head counselor worked day and night to find a living option for Leo to be safe and secure in his family.

A few years later, he visited me at the school to share his exploits since graduation. He admitted to struggling for a year as he determined his next steps, and his aunt eventually asked him to move out, but he found his way and started his own small business. I'm happy to say he is now a well-adjusted young man in a healthy relationship and with a bright future. Once again, I am thankful that this young man is thriving.

I wonder how an administrator from an unhealthy school would have reacted to Leo's plight. He probably would have been placed in a foster home, which could have led to a less-than-positive outcome.

Like Leo's future, I am wondering about my own. Perhaps what lies ahead does not include public high school education. Maybe I will teach at a local community college. Maybe I will continue to write books. Possibly do something outside of education. It feels as if this chapter of my life has come to a close, and I have opened myself to whatever door opens as this one closes.

In recent years, I have wondered whether I was young enough to make a difference in students' lives but decided that wasn't it. I'm not backward, and I'm not burned out. I'm not ready to stop making a difference in today's youth. I am experienced and well-seasoned, and I continually educate myself to be an efficient and effective teacher and mentor. I read and research, searching for exciting and innovatively fun activities that produce scholars who constantly strive to do their best. Some educators might benefit from retiring or looking for other job opportunities when their teaching style doesn't fit with how their students are learning. I refer to these educators as "worksheet enthusiasts." They use more traditional methods like worksheets and less interactive activities, engaging less with their students.

It's important to recognize the hard work of those consistently trying to improve their methods and give their students more dynamic and interesting learning experiences.

So, if the principal sneezes, the whole school gets the cold. Does it make sense now? If the head of the school is lackluster, so is the rest of the school. Because I am an empathetic person, I have been able to get past the overworked and overstressed state of administration, provided that even poor supervision is provided. However, I'm exhausted from waiting for changes to the system that will make it better for both instructors and students.

An exodus of highly qualified, highly trained, and superbly experienced educators has commenced. Actually, I am a bit of a straggler compared to many of my friends who left during the COVID-19 pandemic. I didn't leave because of the well-oiled machine of a team that helped during that time. I didn't leave because the kids needed me. I didn't leave because I could see that my administration was doing everything in its power to support those of us hanging on by the skin of our teeth.

Thousands of instructors have left the profession during and since the COVID-19 pandemic, with more perched to fly the coop. Edweek.org reports that over three hundred thousand teachers left the profession in 2022. Low pay, excessive stress, and inadequate support from administration are common complaints. While pay is vitally important, so is healthy administration. While an unhealthy administration wallows away with tissue in hand and doesn't appear to notice the rest of the school's morale is sick, a healthy administration takes these difficulties and leads with them.

Dear reader, it is time to act and help administrators do their job in a healthy, empowering way. Connect and work with teacher advocacy groups, educate yourself, vote for education-friendly candidates, and become an ambassador for the kind of change you want to see in your schools. Whether you are an educator, administrator, parent, or another type of stakeholder, make a stand and help to keep teachers who make a difference with students in the classroom. Our children are the future, and they deserve the best education that can be supplied.

"There goes my people. I must follow them, for I am their leader."

~ Mahatma Gandhi

Chapter 12

Conclusion

As I close out this memoir of a die-hard quirky high school science teacher, I hope you have laughed with me, cried with me, and stepped into my shoes as I relived the stories of students I have taught and administrators I have worked for. Despite the trials and tribulations, I have succeeded in my endeavors as a passionate, trustworthy, humorous, mindful educator who has provided a safe space and led pupils into the future with problem-solving skills. I love my job, and my students are my job; thus, I love my students.

I love their excitement, their laughter, their innovation. I love that I can laugh, smile, and crack jokes as part of my job-it is never boring. I love to see them make connections and creatively solve problems. I love to see them grow from quiet wallflowers to exuberant leaders, and I love to see them enter high school as children and leave as young adults. I love the personal connections I've made with students and their families. I love my job, and I love my students.

Let's return to the original set of questions at the start of this book. If you had the opportunity to spend time with one of your teachers from your formative years, who would it be? Why? Was it the way they made you feel? Did you feel safe being yourself? What are some of the personality and professional traits of that teacher that helped you feel empowered to learn?

Do you feel a little closer to that person now that you understand the mindset of this teacher? Do you empathize with their woes and hardships? Do you yearn to reach out to them? If so, please do it. It would make that educator beyond happy.

I'd like to think that I cross the minds of previous students from time to time, just as you remember a teacher from your formative years—not for the ego, not for fame, and certainly not for prestige or glory. I'd like to know that I am remembered for making a difference in the lives of thousands of wide-eyed teenagers. Was there something I did that made their lives better at the time? Is there something that transpired during my class that has led them to find a joyful existence? Is there something I did that helped them find something fulfilling as a career?

I would like to think that my years of service have led to positive outcomes for many of those precious minds.

146

Standing at the threshold of my future, I wonder what teachable moments I have learned as I have endured asinine struggles and wonderful adventures in the classroom. I have spent nearly half of my life honing in on skills to be a better teacher, but my students have also guided me. They have taught me much more than I have ever taught them. My students have taught me kindness, tolerance, and acceptance. My students have taught me something new every day, and I have learned how to actively listen and be truly available when a student needs attention. My students have taught me to "think outside of the box" with their creativity, persistence, and hard work. For the last twenty-six years, the students have molded me into who I am today: a proud mama bear.

It has been a challenge to determine the next step in my career. My life's work. My calling. If I leave education, how will this change who I am? Will it change my essence? My being? I like who I am and fear this precipice, this change.

A student asked me recently, "Doc, is everything okay?" I asked him why because it wasn't the first time I had been asked that question that day. He continued, "You don't seem to care as much today. You don't seem like you lately." I changed the subject because it jarred me to the core. How do I respond to this? Is this change in career making me less genuine? Less trustworthy? Less honest? To me, that is terrifying.

Can I remodel the way I see myself? Can I use these fine-tuned skills as a college professor or even online as a teacher who speaks through the screen? How do I share these same exuberant activities and personality traits through soulless media such as the Internet? What can I see myself doing with my talents and time?

Perhaps there are opportunities in the realm of adult education. Perhaps sharing my stories of yesteryear and tomorrow on a larger scale. Maybe I'll become a full-time author and be hired regularly for speaking gigs on the big stage. Perhaps I'll reach out to the author of *From My Heart*, Dr. Neil Hawkes, and train to be a *Values-based* Educator. Or maybe I'll leave education for a different type of employment. There are many maybes in my future at this moment.

During the interim, as I write the conclusion of this memoir, I know in my heart that I will leave public education. My emotions run deep as I toil over this decision, knowing that I will be replaced on the stage of the science classroom. After all, I've been told I'm replaceable.

I just hope that my replacement is as inspiring, passionate, kind, and loving as I have been. The kids deserve that kind of teacher.

Thank you for reading my stories.

**"Our fingerprints don't fade from
the lives we touch."**

~ Judy Blume

About the Author

Dr. Shannon W. McPherson is a highly trained and experienced high school science teacher. She has had twenty-six years of teaching in a wide variety of sciences, including chemistry, advanced placement environmental science, anatomy and physiology, biology, medical microbiology, and pathophysiology. She has also been an adjunct faculty member at a local community college, teaching anatomy and physiology to pre-nursing students. She has taught thousands of students at various levels, which attests to her passion, drive, trustworthiness, and love for her students.

Before teaching, Dr. McPherson was a chiropractor with a growing practice after graduating as salutatorian of her class. While growing her practice, she spent her spare time volunteering at her son's school. During this time, she realized she had missed her calling due to the joy she felt every day as an educator. She pursued and achieved alternative certification to teach science, a field severely lacking teachers. She hasn't looked back since.

A mother of three grown children and a whole pack of grand dogs, she is married and lives outside Houston, Texas. She loves plants, animals, books, writing, and, of course, teaching.

Follow her on her website and blog as she faces a potential transition in her career and continues to share her experiences through the written word.

www.docmcpherson.com

CONTACT THE AUTHOR

Dr. Shannon McPherson is available for consultation, book studies, professional development, speaking engagements, and science teacher mentorship.

For details, please contact her at:

shannonwmcpherson@gmail.com

www.docmcpherson.com